Evaluating and Supporting Early Childhood Teachers

Evaluating and Supporting

Early Childhood

TEACHERS

Redleaf Press®
www.redleafpress.org
800-423-8309

ANGÈLE SANCHO PASSE

Published by Redleaf Press
10 Yorkton Court
St. Paul, MN 55117
www.redleafpress.org

First edition 2015
Cover design by Ryan Scheife, Mayfly Design
Cover illustration by Tumanyan/Shutterstock
Interior design by Percolator Graphic Design
Typeset in Whitman and Ronnia

Excerpts on pages 19, 58–59, 83, and 99 are from NAEYC Code of Ethical Conduct: Supplement for Early Childhood Program Administrators. Copyright © 2011 NAEYC. Reprinted with permission.

Printed in the United States of America
22 21 20 19 18 17 16 15   1 2 3 4 5 6 7 8

Library of Congress Cataloging-in-Publication Data

Passe, Angèle Sancho.
  Evaluating and supporting early childhood teachers / Angèle Sancho Passe.
     pages cm
  Includes bibliographical references.
  ISBN 978-1-60554-366-6 (alk. paper)
  1. Early childhood teachers—Rating of. 2. Early childhood teachers—In-service training.
  3. Mentoring in education. I. Title.
  LB1775.6.P37 2015
     372.11—dc23
                                   2014030735

Printed on acid-free paper

CURR

MIX
Paper from
responsible sources
FSC® C011935

*To all early childhood education teachers, with much respect
and gratitude for their important work*

Contents

3 Recognizing Teacher Quality   39

4 Tools and Techniques for Evaluating Teachers   57

5 *Tools and Techniques for Supporting Teachers*   83

Acknowledgments

I am so grateful for the collective wisdom and support that enable me to think and write on topics that are important and interesting. I wish to thank my family, my team at Redleaf Press, my colleagues in Head Start, and everyone involved in public school systems, child care centers, professional associations, teacher unions, for-profit and nonprofit organizations, faith-based programs, higher education, and government.

A special acknowledgment for the staff, governing board, and members of NAEYC, who lead the way in early childhood education. I am proud to be a part of this forward-thinking community of educators.

A big thank you to Carla Valadez, my editor, who expertly guided the writing of this book.

INTRODUCTION

Just in the last week, I was asked to evaluate the quality of a restaurant where I had lunch, the quality of services at a medical clinic where I had a physical, and the quality of a professional conference I attended. In each case, I was asked to evaluate the way I was treated, the environment, the content of the services, and the skills of the individuals providing the service. Next week, when I take my car for a tune-up, I will no doubt be handed an evaluation form. You are probably having similar experiences. In a data-driven culture like ours, there is a constant striving for measurable improvement. If we can measure it, we can make it better. We can make it better if we measure it. Quality is important.

Evaluation has become part of our everyday lives. We encounter star ratings for hotels, movies, and child care centers. We can find (or write) online reviews for almost any product or service available. We know evaluations have a helpful and productive purpose. They help consumers make smart choices. They allow consumers to provide feedback, which helps the organizations and individuals being evaluated know what to improve. Even in education, the evaluation of children's learning, which helps teachers know what children understand and how they are improving, is now considered essential (Copple and Bredekamp 2009; McAfee, Leong, and Bodrova 2004).

Evaluation of teachers, however, is not yet an accepted idea in the field of education, even among its leaders. As an example, some years ago I was involved in the beginnings of the Quality Improvement Process (QIP) in public schools. It was exciting to work with high-powered administrators and union leaders to apply the research and principles of the quality movement in business to the field of education. It was also frustrating. During a particular meeting about teaching quality, the leaders around the table made a pact not to use the "E" and "A" words, *evaluation* and *accountability*, as if quality improvement could happen without any sort of evaluation. This idea was shortsighted. It set back progress. The thinking that evaluation can be avoided in quality-improvement efforts, however, seems to persist today in early childhood education. I suspect the resistance comes from evaluation being done poorly and from teachers receiving punitive or meaningless evaluation without support to improve.

Resistance to and fears about teacher evaluation are compounded by the growing pressure for quality improvement in education. As never before, policy makers and leaders at local, state, federal, and international levels are focusing on the value of early education in future academic success and even future life success. In the private sector, businesspeople, economists, and journalists are also interested. They know from research that quality of teaching is the biggest factor in the quality of children's learning (Tucker and Stronge 2005). So education in general is under pressure, and teachers are the target. Much attention is being focused on ensuring that early childhood educators improve their teaching.

Education leaders and teachers alike hear assertions such as, "If teachers just did a better job, the children would all learn more and better." And while this statement is true, who is thinking of the teachers? If teachers are doing an unsatisfactory job, *why* is that the case? What do teachers need to be at the top of their form and skills, and are they getting those things? Are they getting coached on their performance, as athletes do, so they can get better? It is unfair to provide minimal support, such as one-time workshops and a yearly box of new materials, and *hope* that quality will improve. I call it the "hope theory" of educational improvement. We hope it works. This is not good enough for children, and it is not good enough for teachers, either. It leaves quality to chance. It makes the field of early childhood education vulnerable to well-meaning but misguided philanthropists, researchers, policy makers, and businesspeople who want to "fix" our practice with their solutions and tools. We jump through the hoops of the latest grant, and we forget to focus on what we need to do for our teachers.

Improving teaching quality, and thus the quality of children's education, is not simply a matter of supplying more materials, more curricula, more training, more rules, more incentives, or more sanctions. Teachers are inundated with new initiatives, but they do not get helpful guidance and support. I believe that education leaders must find a way and a system to support teachers and a way and a system to evaluate them. We need to come up with approaches that make sense for early childhood education. And we have to let go of the idea that teacher evaluation is harmful; when teachers are adequately supported by their leaders, evaluation isn't a threat, it's an opportunity for collaboration, growth, and improvement.

WHY I WROTE THIS BOOK

My interest in this topic comes from several perspectives in my career as a teacher, union activist, administrator, teacher educator, organization development consultant, and coach. Over the years, I have had many professional conversations about teacher skills with other educators, leaders, and researchers. Too often I hear that while supporting teachers is a good thing, evaluating them is too punitive. Teachers will simply "do what is right," once they understand what needs to be done. I agree that teachers will try to do what's right. I am also aware that the lack of a good system for teacher evaluation has created problems in K–12 education. For example, ineffective teachers who did not receive proper evaluations and support prevented children from learning even close to what they were capable of learning (Sanders and Rivers 1996). I don't want to replicate this condition in early childhood education. Addressing best practices in teacher evaluation and support is crucial in our efforts to improve education quality for children. Evaluation cannot be a forbidden word or a scary practice.

In the child care field, turnover rate is very high, comparable to that of fast-food restaurants. In elementary education, one-third of new teachers leave the profession within the first three years. At the same time, new people are attracted to the field every day, people with varying levels of skill and experience who need support to make their way in the profession.

Fears of teacher evaluation and high attrition rates are symptoms of larger problems in early childhood education: inadequate systems of evaluation and support. These are problems I hope to help solve in this book. As a leader in education, you will find that you already have many of the skills and tools you need to effectively evaluate and support teachers. This is especially true if you have been a classroom teacher yourself. You already know how to assess and support children. The process will be similar when assessing and supporting the adults you serve.

WHO THIS BOOK IS FOR

Throughout the book, I use the term *education leader* to refer to any individual who has a role in evaluating and supporting teachers. Education leaders include child care center directors, program managers, and school principals, who serve as both supervisors and leaders. These leaders have the responsibility of hiring and firing teachers and, therefore, of evaluating and supporting them too. Education leaders also include peer teachers with leadership, but no supervisory, responsibilities, such as team leaders, education coordinators, consultants, mentors, coaches, lead teachers, and educators with other related job titles. Even though evaluation is usually reserved for the leaders who are the supervisors, support is considered part of every leader's job. Both functions are essential. For the purpose of this book, I am going to point to the overlap and the importance of each function. All education leaders will benefit from the ideas and strategies in this book, but you will need to decide your own parameters for implementing the strategies, based on your role within your organization and your organization's human resources system.

HOW THE BOOK IS ORGANIZED

I have organized the book so that later chapters build upon information in earlier chapters, but you can read the information in any order that makes sense to you:

- Chapter 1 addresses your role and responsibilities as an education leader who evaluates and supports teachers in your program.

- Chapter 2 provides suggestions for creating a caring community of workers, setting the groundwork for a positive workplace environment in which evaluation and support practices can thrive.

- Chapter 3 strives to define *teaching quality*, pointing to authoritative resources on the topic and revealing how these resources can help you prepare to evaluate teachers.

- Chapter 4 digs deeper into the topic of evaluation, providing specific tools and techniques for implementing evaluations—from planning the evaluations to communicating results to teachers.

- Chapter 5 presents strategies, tools, and techniques for supporting teachers—including coaching, counseling, and mentoring—using the data gathered from evaluations.

- Chapter 6 addresses differentiating and scaffolding support based on the unique needs of your group and individual teachers.

- Chapter 7 helps you create an evaluation and support plan for your center, school, or team.

Throughout the chapters, I invite you to follow education leaders Sara, Monique, and Jon on their journeys in evaluating and supporting teachers. Their actions and reactions to scenarios in their settings are based on my own observations of education leaders in the field and on best practices in human resource development. You'll learn from their challenges and successes.

SARA, *Center Director*

Sara is the director of a child care center. She has been a director for ten years and feels that she is good at her job. Her center has a high staff-turnover rate, especially in the assistant teacher group. Sara's center has six lead teachers for two infant classrooms, two toddler classrooms, and two preschool rooms. Four of the lead teachers have bachelor's degrees and two have Child Development Associate (CDA) credentials. Her center is seeking NAEYC accreditation. It is also part of the state's quality initiative. The center has a Quality Rating and Improvement System (QRIS) rating of three stars, and Sara has a goal of obtaining four stars within the next year. She feels confident in her ability to lead her staff, but she is challenged by teachers who are resistant to suggestions and by the frequent changes in staffing. ∎

MONIQUE, *Education Coordinator and Coach*

Monique is an education coordinator and coach in a Head Start program. She does not have supervisory responsibilities, but she is in a leadership position. She oversees five classrooms in three buildings. Her job is to ensure the curriculum is implemented, the children are learning, and the teaching staff (lead teachers and assistants) does all there is to do. When her director approached her with the idea of becoming an education coach, she was excited. She always wanted to boost the quality of instruction in her program. She also felt worried, because she had attended coaching workshops before, and while she had learned a lot, the whole approach seemed overwhelming. She has a solid knowledge of early childhood education and good interpersonal skills, but she does not yet have the vocabulary nor the structure to organize a coaching plan for the classroom staff. ∎

JON, *Principal*

Jon is the principal of a public elementary school. His district began a pre-K to third grade initiative last year, and, as a result, he has two pre-K classrooms in his building. He has no experience with pre-K. As an elementary principal, he had not even considered K–3 as part of early childhood education until recently. He likes the idea of serving younger children and is looking forward to this new "pre-K–3 alignment" as a benefit to children. He still finds the arrangement to be somewhat stressful. He now has a leadership role in an area where he has no expertise. He worries that the newly hired pre-K teachers will do their own thing and not listen to him. ∎

Also included throughout the book are checklists, self-assessments, and reproducible forms designed to aid your planning. As you experiment with these tools, feel free to modify them for your own use; you know your situation best. Reproducible versions of these forms can be found in the appendix. At the end of each chapter, you will find reflection questions to help you think critically about evaluating and supporting teachers. Reflect on your own or discuss these questions with your staff or professional learning community.

This book focuses on the pressing issue of evaluation and support of teachers, and it provides solutions. Evaluation means nothing if a system of support is not in place to promote growth and improvement. Evaluation without support is like testing children without making plans to teach them the skills they need to be successful. I know together we can improve teacher evaluation and support. Use principles and strategies I describe in this book to get started on this important work.

1 THE ROLE *of the* EDUCATION LEADER

You have the job of evaluating and supporting teachers. Either you have willingly applied for the job or you have been selected by your organization because someone thought you would be good at it. Are you a supervisor, principal, director, manager, coordinator, coach, mentor, or lead teacher? Regardless of your title, you are an education leader. You have the big responsibility to create and maintain a quality workforce of educators and, ultimately, to support a quality education for children.

The main resources of a child care center or school are its human resources, and teachers are the most important element. The quality of teachers and their practices are directly affected by the quality of supervision and management, which in turn affects the quality of children's education. The pyramid below illustrates how the education children receive is buttressed by the leadership and management, the teachers themselves, and the teaching (instruction and curriculum). If these three elements are good, then a high-quality education for children will happen.

The education leader's responsibility, then, is to ensure that each section of the pyramid is:

1. functioning at a high-quality level (which requires monitoring through evaluation) and

2. improving or maintaining its quality level (which requires a strong and intentional system of support).

DEFINING *EVALUATION* AND *SUPPORT*

Evaluation has two definitions with distinctive nuances. One is to "judge the worth of" and the other is "to find the value of." I suspect the resistance to the idea of evaluating teachers comes from the first meaning. Teachers are good people who care for children. It seems harsh to pass judgment on them. So I want to focus on the second meaning. It is important for us to find the value in teachers and to reflect it back to them. It is also important for teachers to find their own value and nurture it.

Support has four possible meanings:

1. to hold up from beneath,

2. to uphold,

3. to stand by, and

4. to provide for.

Some synonymous verbs are

- *bolster,*
- *shore up,*
- *promote,*
- *encourage,*
- *strengthen,*
- *second,*
- *attend to,*
- *reinforce,* and
- *keep from falling.*

These words give an image of what best practices for supporting teachers might be. I want you to keep the images in your head as you continue to read.

Teaching young children is a difficult job. First, it is physically demanding. Teachers must lift and carry babies and toddlers; sit on the floor or on small chairs all day long, even for meals; and care for the physical and safety needs of young children. Second, it is intellectually and emotionally demanding.

Teachers have to constantly put themselves in the minds of their learners. These little learners are developmentally far from adult reasoning and behaviors. The kindergarten teacher has to think like a five-year-old in order to find the right activities, materials, pace, and safety measures. And not just for one five-year-old, but twenty of them! The teacher of fifteen-month-old Sofia not only has to know that climbing on the shelf is developmentally appropriate but also that the toddler still needs to be stopped. The teacher of nine-month-old Alex has to understand that his crying is due to separation anxiety, and her job is to comfort both the baby and his mother—because teaching young children means working with the parents of children too. Adding parents to the mix makes the job even more challenging.

Teachers who started with hope and good intentions are leaving for other jobs at a fast rate, both in the private sector and in public schools. The main reason for dissatisfaction on the job is the lack of professional and emotional support. Teachers feel alone. They feel that they are on their own against all the pressures of the job. Even if they work in teams, the majority of their time is spent interacting with little people who have limited vocabularies, are egocentric, and are learning self-control. They do feel depleted at the end of the day!

Instead of ignoring or adding to teachers' challenging daily work, feelings of isolation, and exhaustion, let's evaluate and support them. Let's find the value in teachers and reflect it back to them. Let's hold up and stand by teachers. Let's encourage and strengthen them.

INTRODUCING THE GUIDING PRINCIPLES FOR EVALUATING AND SUPPORTING TEACHERS

The field of early childhood education can be proud of having good research in child development and developmentally appropriate practices. We have enough information to have top-quality classrooms, but we are missing an aspect of the equation that prevents us from applying that information most effectively. We have not figured out a way to evaluate and support teachers that is calm, clear, consistent, and effective; we are not adequately measuring or nurturing teachers' growth, which means we are limiting the quality of education for children.

One of the reasons for this problem may be that many education leaders start out as teachers and move through the ranks with little or no training on how to adequately evaluate and support adult teachers. Even so, education leaders have a wealth of knowledge from their experience as (or with) teachers. What if we use the principles that teachers use to support children's learning to support teachers' growth and development? What if we use a parallel process and treat teachers the same way we want them to treat children? I don't mean to oversimplify the issue. Teachers are adults, and their adult needs and characteristics have to be taken into consideration, but we can adapt what we know about teaching children to create a process for supporting teachers for maximum effectiveness. What is good for the children is good for the teachers.

This concept of a parallel process for supporting teachers has always made sense to me. I have honed it through my studies in early education, adult education, and organization development, and through my work as a teacher of children and of teachers, an administrator, a coach, and an advocate for quality. I believe that the alignment of organizational development, adult professional development, and child development is crucial to quality in education. A calm and efficient organization begets a calm and effective teacher begets calm and learning children.

In this spirit, and using *Developmentally Appropriate Practice in Early Childhood Programs Serving Children from Birth through Age 8* (Copple and Bredekamp 2009) as our guide, I suggest five guiding principles for evaluating and supporting teachers that parallel what teachers are expected to do with children.

Five Guiding Principles for Educating Children and for Evaluating and Supporting Teachers

CHILDREN GET A QUALITY EDUCATION WHEN TEACHERS . . .	EARLY CHILDHOOD TEACHERS GET QUALITY PROFESSIONAL EVALUATION AND SUPPORT WHEN LEADERS . . .
1. Create a caring community of learners	1. Create a caring community of workers
2. Enhance development and learning	2. Enhance professional competence
3. Plan an appropriate curriculum	3. Provide appropriate direction and resources
4. Assess development	4. Assess professional skills and growth
5. Develop reciprocal relationships with families	5. Facilitate involvement in the field of early childhood education

Copple and Bredekamp 2009, 16–23

As you follow the ideas in the book, these five guiding principles for supporting and evaluating teachers will come to life. But before we jump into the important work of evaluation and support, let's take a moment for reflection. Let's identify what you are already doing well in your daily work of evaluating and supporting teachers, as well as what areas might need improvement.

ASSESSING YOUR CURRENT PRACTICES

We expect teachers to reflect on their practices in order to meet the needs of children. It is important for leaders to reflect too. Use the two tools that follow to help you examine the current situation in your center or school. The first (see page 12) is a quick observation tool to assess your teachers' behaviors and practices. The second (see page 13) is a self-assessment to help you evaluate your own behaviors and practices. Reproducible versions of both tools can be found in the appendix. The checklist items on the tools illustrate behaviors and actions that should be evident for each guiding principle. The results will reveal how well you are currently following the guiding principles and provide some clues about how your behaviors and practices may affect your work of evaluation and support.

◆ ◆ ◆

How did you do with these quick surveys? First, congratulate yourself on the items you answered with "always" and "usually" in either survey! You and your program are on the right track here. Did you reply "always" or "usually" for every statement under any of the guiding principle categories on both forms? If so, you are likely following that guiding principle consistently in your practice. Keep it up!

Second, focus on the items you answered with "sometimes" and "never" on the forms. These are areas that need improvement. In these areas, evaluation and support are not consistently happening well. Take note of any patterns in your answers under particular guiding principles. Which principle appears to need the most improvement?

Now compare the answers from the observation of teachers' behaviors and your self-assessment. Analyze their similarities. Do you see a connection between what the teachers do and what you do? For example, do the teachers listen to one another? Do you listen to them? Do the teachers understand and

Observation: How Well Are Teachers Evaluated and Supported?

Read the statements below and then for about a week observe what teachers say and do during their daily interactions. Checkmark the appropriate box to indicate whether the statements are true for your teachers always, usually, sometimes, or never.

In my program, teachers . . .	ALWAYS	USUALLY	SOMETIMES	NEVER
Create a caring community of workers				
1. Greet one another every day.	☐	☐	☐	☐
2. Smile and make positive comments.	☐	☐	☐	☐
3. Assist one another with personal and professional issues.	☐	☐	☐	☐
4. Listen to one another.	☐	☐	☐	☐
Enhance professional competence				
5. Integrate previous experience with new knowledge received in professional development.	☐	☐	☐	☐
6. Know how to assess and analyze children's learning.	☐	☐	☐	☐
7. Know the impact of their teaching.	☐	☐	☐	☐
8. Are organized and intentional in their planning.	☐	☐	☐	☐
Receive appropriate direction				
9. Know what quality is in our organization.	☐	☐	☐	☐
10. Understand and articulate the expectations and objectives of our organization.	☐	☐	☐	☐
11. Make educational choices based on program objectives.	☐	☐	☐	☐
Assess skills and growth				
12. Assess their own teaching.	☐	☐	☐	☐
13. Take risks, try new ideas, and evaluate them.	☐	☐	☐	☐
14. Cooperate with and encourage one another, sharing spaces, materials, and ideas.	☐	☐	☐	☐
Facilitate involvement in the field of early childhood education				
15. Mentor one another.	☐	☐	☐	☐
16. Are connected to the early childhood education professional community.	☐	☐	☐	☐
17. Share their professional interests and enthusiasm with colleagues.	☐	☐	☐	☐

Self-Assessment: How Well Are You Evaluating and Supporting Teachers?

Read the statements below and then reflect on your own daily interactions. Checkmark the appropriate box to indicate whether the statements are true for you always, usually, sometimes, or never.

In my program, I . . .

	ALWAYS	USUALLY	SOMETIMES	NEVER
Create a caring community of workers				
1. Greet teachers every day with a positive comment.	☐	☐	☐	☐
2. Smile, laugh, and am enthusiastic about our work with children, families, and colleagues.	☐	☐	☐	☐
3. Provide comfort and assistance for personal and professional issues.	☐	☐	☐	☐
4. Help resolve problems.	☐	☐	☐	☐
5. Listen.	☐	☐	☐	☐
Enhance professional competence				
6. Give specific affirmations on performance.	☐	☐	☐	☐
7. Give feedback when teaching is going well.	☐	☐	☐	☐
8. Give feedback when teaching is not going well.	☐	☐	☐	☐
9. Provide professional development to the group and to individuals.	☐	☐	☐	☐
Provide appropriate direction and resources				
10. Communicate clear direction and objectives in multiple ways.	☐	☐	☐	☐
11. Am consistent with consequences.	☐	☐	☐	☐
12. Use effective questions to encourage reflective practice.	☐	☐	☐	☐
13. Provide information and resources.	☐	☐	☐	☐
Assess skills and growth				
14. Assess classroom quality.	☐	☐	☐	☐
15. Assess teacher skills.	☐	☐	☐	☐
16. Scaffold teacher skills.	☐	☐	☐	☐
17. Encourage teachers to persist even when the work is challenging.	☐	☐	☐	☐
Facilitate involvement in the field of early childhood education				
18. Help teachers feel connected to the early childhood education professional community.	☐	☐	☐	☐
19. Engage teachers actively in making decisions for our center.	☐	☐	☐	☐
20. Share the teachers' interests and enthusiasm.	☐	☐	☐	☐

articulate the expectations and objectives of your organization? Do you provide clear direction? Do the teachers assess their own skills? Do you assess their skills and provide scaffolding?

Patterns in behaviors and practices are likely because leaders set the tone in their organizations. Think again about the parallel process. Children cannot learn what we don't teach them. Teachers cannot perform at their peak if we don't give clear guidance and support. It is not just about being a role model; it is about being intentional in demonstrating what to do and how to do it. If you greet teachers every day, they are more likely to greet one another. If you give them specific affirmations on performance and assess their skills, they are more likely to know the impact of their teaching.

If the answers between the two surveys do not match up nicely, there may be a disconnect between your expectations for teachers and your actions, or a disconnect between your good intentions and the systems in place to support those intentions. For example, years ago I was called in to help a center with many "behavior issues." In this preschool setting of four- and five-year-olds, the children were not attentive and were bickering constantly. They would run out of the room despite special doorknobs to prevent them from opening the door. The center director had provided several workshops on behavior management for the teachers, but the children's behavior was not improving. She was getting very frustrated with the teachers, and she let them know how disappointed she was in the continued behavior problems. The teachers were angry with both the director and with the "terrible" children. They started ignoring the director's suggestions for fixing behavior because the strategies never seemed to work. They blamed families for poor parenting. They called in sick frequently and accused one another of not pulling their weight. When I arrived on the scene, I was asked to fix the people—the children, the teachers, the director, and the parents.

After observing the center in action, however, I noticed that the curriculum was designed for toddlers, not for children bound for kindergarten. The center had grown from an infant-toddler program to a center that included pre-kindergarten rooms without carefully considering a developmentally appropriate curriculum for older children. The activities were not engaging or stimulating for the children, and so the children acted out. The problems were ultimately caused by problems in the systems of evaluation and support: a lack of clear direction in explaining the change to pre-K; no assessment of pre-K teaching skills (the director did not know her staff wasn't teaching to the children's level); and no professional development geared toward a developmentally appropriate curriculum for preschoolers. The problems were not in the people.

They all wanted to do the right thing, but they did not have a system to help them do that. The leader had good intentions, but she was not effective in her efforts. If the responses on your observation and self-assessment forms differ greatly, consider whether the systems and actions you employ are consistent with your hopes and intentions.

As you work to implement a system of evaluation and support in your setting, continue to reflect on your practices, behaviors, intentions, actions, and systems, as well as the behaviors and practices of your teachers. Think about the strengths and weaknesses and inconsistencies revealed by the two assessments in this section. By the end of the book, you will have a plan for improvement! You might even retake the two assessments again in several months after you apply the ideas in the chapters that follow to see how far you've come and to refocus your efforts on the guiding principles.

VISUALIZING YOUR WELL-SUPPORTED AND WELL-EVALUATED EARLY CHILDHOOD WORKPLACE

You know supporting and evaluating teachers is your responsibility, and you have five guiding principles to provide direction for your efforts. Now I want to give you a glimpse of what you're working toward, what a workplace feels like for teachers when their leaders follow each of the guiding principles. This will help you think further about your own job and responsibilities. I hope it will motivate you to get started on the challenging but important work of evaluation and support.

Create a Caring Community of Workers

Teachers who are supported get to know one another's personalities, interests, and abilities. They have opportunities to problem solve, resolve conflicts, and communicate often. The atmosphere is respectful of their differences. Communication happens in many ways: in writing, in person, by e-mail, in large groups, in small groups, and individually. The leaders pay attention to what's being said through the grapevine, the informal communication that happens in the parking lot or staff room. Teachers feel free to check their assumptions directly. They do not engage in gossip. They help one another and collaborate to achieve joint goals for children's learning. The educators in a caring community feel free to be creative, be curious, and develop their competence.

Enhance Professional Competence

Teachers who are supported feel their performance is evaluated fairly. Their struggles and efforts are acknowledged. Teachers get feedback and scaffolding to continue to improve. They see demonstrations of good practices in person or in videos. They receive information in formal settings, such as in trainings, and in informal ways, such as through handouts in their inboxes about an issue that they have been wondering about. Training is not one-size-fits-all. Experienced teachers, who may be restless in their position, get new challenges, such as having time in their schedules to research new curriculum materials for the center or to mentor new teachers. Novice teachers get explicit direction so they can practice new skills without the burden of too many decisions. They all feel encouraged to keep trying and to keep improving.

Provide Appropriate Direction and Resources

Teachers who are supported work in an organization that has a plan and explains this plan. They know what the goals are for children, for families, and for the program. They can see their own role in this plan. There are no surprises. Teachers hear about new initiatives in the early stages. They are not able to cancel an initiative, but they have a voice in how to implement it, and their leaders listen. Discussions are held to modify the timeline or get more training. Periodic reviews and updates keep everyone in the loop. Clear direction helps everyone understand what to do.

Assess Professional Skills and Growth

Teachers who are supported are aware of the tools used to observe and assess their classrooms. These tools might include informal checklists or formal validated tools to assess the dynamics in the classroom and the teaching skills of the teachers. In either case, the teachers know what the assessments contain and use them to do self-assessments so they can compare their perceptions with those of the observers. They have confidence in the evaluation system. They accept observations or videotaping as tools for reviewing and growing their skills. They understand the cause and effect relationship between their actions and the learning and behaviors of children. They engage in deep discussions about how to make changes to their teaching so children learn more. They know that the purpose of assessment is to make a plan for children's learning and to make a plan for their own professional growth.

Facilitate Involvement in the Field of Early Childhood Education

Teachers who are supported do not feel isolated. They realize they are part of a professional movement. They have opportunities to participate in formal events such as conferences, where they can meet colleagues from other organizations. They also have a system in their own center or school to share ideas or expertise. This may happen in a book club, reading the same book about infant activities and sharing ideas informally. Or it may be an official study group, meeting once a month for a year to explore a topic. Teachers know their work is a part of an effort that is larger than themselves; they feel a part of the effort.

◆ ◆ ◆

I hope you find these descriptions encouraging. They describe a positive environment where people work hard and feel good about it. When evaluation and support go hand in hand, the teachers and the climate of your setting will benefit. Most importantly, the children will benefit. I visit and observe many centers, programs, and schools. I can tell how things are going from what I see and hear in the hallways. When teachers treat children harshly, I know that the teachers are not getting good evaluation and support. I can also tell the kind of direction and support teachers are getting when I look at the test scores. Low student achievement is always coupled with low adult direction, and low morale. The opposite is true. When children are doing well, there is a parallel sense of success for teachers. They know their value. They are confident in their abilities.

Teachers cannot do their complicated work alone. They should be able to count on their leaders to support their professional growth with care, empathy, and a solid sense of direction.

JON, *Principal*

Jon was observing Ms. Ana's reading group. She was reading *Goldilocks and the Three Bears*. As she began the story, four-year-old Mason started to whimper. Ms. Ana asked him to stop crying so the children could hear the story. Mason continued to whimper. She told him to go to the time-out chair to calm down. On his way there, Mason kicked the puzzle table and all the pieces went flying. Irritated, Ms. Ana helped him sit in the time-out chair, went back to the group, and closed the book saying, "I will not read today, too much disruption."

Jon was less concerned about Ms. Ana's specific behavior with Mason than about her beliefs about reading to children. Early literacy is a major objective of the school. He had seen Ms. Ana stop her readings other times, and he was concerned that the children were missing educational

cont'd

opportunities. They were not getting the instruction promised. Through the process of several discussions Jon clarified Ms. Ana's beliefs about reading and about behavior during reading. They talked about the cause and effect of various actions she had taken. They looked at the children's data and saw that their language scores were low, a sign that they needed more reading. They explored the consequences of not reading to the whole class when one child was not complying. Then they started to plan intentionally. They talked about not stopping readings and having options to help disruptive children. It was indeed a longer process than a simple directive, but it led to a long-term solution. In the end, Ms. Ana's skills improved. It was not magic. Jon was instrumental in helping her grow as an excellent early childhood professional. ■

Reflection Questions

1. Review your answers from the observation and self-assessment forms on pages 12–13. Think about your role as an education leader who wants to evaluate and support teachers. What parts will be easy for you to accomplish? What parts will be challenging?

2. Lead a discussion with your staff on the meaning of *quality support for teachers*. What does it mean for your group? Make a list of behaviors and actions. Compare the list to the five guiding principles described in this chapter.

2 CREATING *a* CARING COMMUNITY *of* WORKERS

Early childhood program administrators are managers with the responsibility for providing oversight for all program operations, as well as serving as leaders in early childhood in early care and education programs. They are responsible for creating a caring, cooperative workplace that respects human dignity, promotes professional satisfaction, and models positive relationships.

—NAEYC, *NAEYC Code of Ethical Conduct:*
Supplement for Early Childhood Program Administrators

We expect teachers to create a caring community of learners in their classrooms. Following a parallel process and the first guiding principle, education leaders need to create a caring community of workers. The groundwork for this caring community must be set *before* evaluations take place, because evaluating teachers can only happen effectively when leaders establish trust and teachers feel safe giving and receiving feedback. You can start developing your caring community by creating good working conditions, setting a common agenda, developing professional relationships, nurturing a culture of collaboration, communicating effectively, and modeling caring and empathy. In a caring community of workers, positive relationships develop among teachers and between leaders and teachers. Leaders and teachers rally together around joint goals for improving the quality of children's education.

CREATING GOOD WORKING CONDITIONS

Working conditions span physical and emotional areas. Under physical conditions, I include fair compensation, a clean and safe environment, and a predictable schedule with reasonable flexibility. Under emotional conditions, I include an emotionally safe environment where respectful behaviors and language are used, an environment free of meanness and criticism. One of the first steps in generating good working conditions begins before a teacher even sets foot in your setting—in careful hiring.

Hire with Care

Hiring is one of the most important steps in building and supporting a caring staff overall. The qualities and skills of the people hired will make a big impact on the team. A new teacher will either contribute to or detract from your caring community. She might fit in easily and have the right competencies, or she might not. If you know you will not have the time or patience to provide remedial assistance to an inexperienced candidate, don't consider hiring someone who doesn't have the necessary skills—even if you like her personality.

You may decide to hire someone for the good personal qualities she has, even though her technical skills are low. This often happens in programs that need teachers who speak a language other than English. They may be nice community members who work well with children and parents but do not have literate language skills. In this case, be prepared and willing to provide this teacher with appropriate professional development to be effective and confident. This person needs to become a productive member of the larger team, and she can only do so with your help.

In our field, we tend to be generous and want to give people the benefit of the doubt. During an interview, if you find yourself wondering if a person will work out as part of the team—because of some lack of technical qualifications or professional behaviors—listen to your feelings. They are probably right.

Pay Fairly

Once teachers are hired, pay them as fairly as you can. According to the best practices described in the Program Administration Scale (PAS) designed by Teri Talan and Paula Jorde Bloom (2004), an excellent program needs to have an equitable salary scale including merit increases. It also should have a compensation plan that offers twelve sick leave and fifteen or more vacation days per year. You may not be able to set the wages or benefits for your organization, but be mindful of the pay standards in your area. Early childhood teachers recognize that they are not in a lucrative field, but they appreciate and deserve fairness.

The wage issue is a matter of great debate and anguish in the field of early childhood education (Zaslow 2011). Do what you can to work on wage fairness at your site with whatever resources you have, and then consider advocating for long-range solutions at the public policy level.

Set a Predictable Schedule with Reasonable Flexibility

Taking care of the children is priority number one, and providing children with consistent care from consistent educators is part of that task. Work with teachers to set a predictable schedule, but once that schedule is set, realize they will need flexibility at times to accommodate their own lives and families. It's okay to be understanding. And being reasonably flexible shows you trust teachers and respect that they have lives outside of the workplace.

You can find many ways to accommodate teachers' schedules. You might arrange for a teacher to take shorter breaks on a day when she needs to leave early. You might arrange to combine classrooms for a short time or have an administrator cover the room to accommodate a teacher who needs to leave early. These solutions should be made equitably and openly, so everyone feels they can have a turn. You might say, "Today, Susie needs to leave twenty minutes early. I will cover for her during that time, just like I did for Tammy last week." Organize the schedule and arrangements for relief far enough in advance so teachers and administrators can plan their time accordingly.

Create a Physically and Emotionally Safe Environment

Cleanliness and safety are basic requirements for children's spaces. The same goes for adult spaces such as staff room, bathrooms, and offices. Teachers need to have a place for personal belongings and adult-size furniture. Everyone is responsible for maintaining the environment, but it is not the teachers' job to do the upkeep. Be alert to the environment and provide or advocate for any necessary repairs and maintenance to the workplace.

The social environment of a center or school also contributes to a teacher's sense of safety. The workplace can be ripe with gossip and tension. Adults work closely with one another and parents. They share intimate details about one another's lives. Express high expectations for positive behavior in the workplace, and monitor the climate of your setting closely for complaints, negative comments, bullying, or hearsay so you can address them immediately in private.

SETTING A COMMON AGENDA

All teachers want children to do well. All leaders want teachers to do well. As a community of workers, you and your teachers can agree on this as the first assumption of setting a common agenda: everyone wants the best for the adults or children they serve. Teachers follow the standards for learning because they are the *best* for children; teachers and leaders adhere to a code of ethical conduct because it is the *best* for children, teachers, families, and administrators. These are the big-picture motivators for our work.

From there, however, we have the daily work to address. Sometimes we aim too far and too broadly in our goals. For example, when I ask teachers what they want for children, they say they want each to have a happy and healthy future. I agree with that hope, but early childhood teachers cannot control the next many years of a child's life. Instead, I recommend crafting a common agenda around the daily work you and the teachers do with children and with one another. As a community of workers, you and your teachers can then rally together around this agenda and unite to find creative and effective ways to achieve these joint goals.

To craft your agenda, think more about what you want to see happen now, every day of the week, every hour of the day in your program. And ask your staff what they want to see happen. Use the questions in the left column of the table on the next page to help you and your staff establish your agenda items. Example goals that might come out of these probing questions are included in the right column of the table. If these ideas appear down to earth, that's the intention. You and your teachers are busy, and I want you to have a practical agenda.

As you establish a common agenda with your teachers, know that teachers need their leaders to *consistently* maintain and support these joint goals for children's learning. Sometimes we say we have the same goals as teachers, but then we make those goals difficult to implement. For example, to support teachers in achieving a goal, you might send them to be trained on best practices for teaching toddlers, but if you maintain a less than optimal adult–child ratio in your setting, you hinder teachers' abilities to accomplish what they learned. Or after attending a workshop on early literacy, your teachers might come back with new ideas, such as making books accessible to all children, to support your literacy goals. But if your center has a policy that books need to be on high shelves except during scheduled story times, these new ideas can never be implemented. One reason for these inconsistencies in joint goals and leaders' actions may be ignorance: if leaders don't attend workshops with teachers, they don't learn about best practices and may be challenged to support new ideas. Or it may be economic: leaders want to save money, and having fewer staff members means

Setting a Common Agenda

QUESTION: WHAT DO WE WANT?	ANSWER: OUR AGENDA
What do we want to see happen during [arrival, meal time, circle time, departure]?	We want calm meals with conversation. At mealtime all adults will sit at the table with a small group of children. The teachers will serve the food to the children. They make conversation with the children.
What would make our work productive—or easier—during these times?	The food will be ready and in the middle of tables before children and adults sit down. Extra paper and sponges for emergency cleanup of spills will be ready so adults can remain at the table.
What do we want children to learn? [Follow our state learning standards, parents' requests, children's interests]	We will review the early childhood standards of our state, focusing on social-emotional development, specifically "ability to share feelings verbally." We will use the social-emotional curriculum we purchased once a week for a lesson. We will use the techniques every day to reinforce the concepts.
What are our team's preferred communication methods? How will we continue?	We will have a weekly meeting for fifteen minutes on Monday. We will evaluate how it is going after three weeks and make changes if we need to.

fewer expenses. In either case, when teachers detect contradictions between the team goals and their daily reality, the result is cynicism and distrust—which does not support a caring community of workers.

DEVELOPING PROFESSIONAL RELATIONSHIPS WITH TEACHERS

An early childhood program is a cauldron of relationships: children to adults, children to children, and adults to adults. There is no escaping the charged atmosphere. It can be all smiles and happy high fives one minute and screaming and crying the next minute. Just as teachers build relationships with children in order to best support their learning and development, leaders must build relationships with teachers to best foster professional growth. Doing so will also establish trust, a necessary element in a caring community.

Sometimes the word *relationship* is misunderstood in a professional setting. Developing a relationship is interpreted as becoming personal friends with teachers and creating the kind of bond that's formed during happy hour events or by exchanging holiday gifts. This is not the kind of relationship I am proposing.

Education leaders need to form *professional* relationships with teachers, not necessarily personal ones. A professional relationship is one based on common professional goals, such as the common agenda discussed earlier, whereas a personal relationship is based on common interests or personalities.

When I first began my work in coaching teachers, an elementary coach and I were discussing the timing issue around building relationships. She said, "I feel like I spend six months building the relationship. By then, it is already March, and most of the school year is over. In the meantime, I am friendly and provide tons of resources. Sometimes I model best practices by taking over the classroom for a lesson. I even bring teachers a latte once in a while. They all say I am really helpful, but I do not see much change happening in the classroom."

Resources and lattes are not enough. And waiting until March to form productive relationships with teachers is not acceptable for the children. If the goal of developing relationships is to help teachers better educate children, then that goal is lost if there are no results. I believe that education leaders can develop professional relationships with teachers *starting on the first day*, even if they do not develop friendships. They can be friendly to teachers, of course, but leaders must use the goal to develop the relationship, rather than developing the relationship and then pursuing the goal.

MONIQUE, *Education Coordinator and Coach*

Monique was assigned to coach teacher Jill. Jill was somewhat resistant at first. She felt the new literacy initiative was just a new fad, soon to be replaced by another bright idea. All the children seemed to be doing just fine, and she did not see the point of spending extra time with Monique to discuss her classroom. Jill and Monique had basically ignored each other in the normal course of their work in the past three years. Monique was nervous about how to build a relationship with Jill to begin their work together.

The training Monique attended to prepare herself as a coach had a clear formula to support teachers and help them be as effective as possible: look at children's data, ask questions, and listen. And that is what she did. Very early on, they looked at children's data. Monica videotaped children when she observed the classroom, and she and Jill looked at the videos side by side. They looked at the results of children's assessment together, again, side by side. In fact, they rarely, if ever, sat across from each other. They always sat side by side, literally putting their heads together to look at data about children's learning. This is how Monique and Jill built their relationship. They focused on the children, not each other and their personalities. This relationship is not about Monique and Jill. It is about the children. ■

Use Data as the Basis of the Relationship

Relationship-based interactions can be formalized immediately, without waiting for them to develop on their own. Monique and Jill's story is not simplistic, though it is fairly simple. Monique built a professional relationship with Jill using a practical and effective strategy: she made data the basis of the relationship.

What is data in early childhood education? Data is everything that we know about the children, the classroom environment, and the teaching interactions with children. Use this data to foster productive, collaborative, and solutions-focused conversations with teachers. The following are examples of data you can use to foster your professional relationships:

- **Child observations notes.** These notes capture what children do or do not do. The simplest items are written notes about what the observer sees the children do in the classroom. Together, you and the teacher can analyze observational notes over time and try to figure out the patterns. For example, if you contrasted these two notes about circle time, you and the teacher could identify the difference in the experiences, theorize the cause, and come up with a solution to create a more consistent circle time experience for children:

  —During circle time, all the children are attentive to the story. Several respond to the questions and make comments about the pictures. Circle time is ten minutes long.

  —During circle time, some children are not attentive to the story. Several children get up and wander away. One child makes comments about the pictures in the book. Circle time is twenty-five minutes long.

- **Photographs or examples of children's work.** Examples of student work may be drawings, scribbling or writing samples, artwork, dictations, or pictures of structures children have built in the block area. Together, you and the teacher might compare children's work to the early childhood standards for the age group or to specific goals you've established for each child. From there, you could help the teacher come up with ideas on how to help each child develop more advanced skills.

- **Videos of children in action.** Videos only need to be about three to ten minutes long to illustrate a situation. You and the teacher might review the videos together and discuss children's behavior.

> ### JON, *Principal*
> Jon videotaped children during a circle time reading. At the beginning of circle time, the teacher did not have the book ready and spent about three to four minutes looking for it. By the time she found it, three children had left circle. During the reading, several children lost attention. The story was long and complicated. Jon just videotaped the children's behaviors during the reading, not the teacher's behavior. When he and the teacher viewed the video clip together, they discussed the children's behaviors. What were they doing? Why were they acting this way? By focusing on the children, the teacher did not feel targeted personally. That made her receptive to viewing her role in the situation. It helped her come to the question, what can I do to change children's behavior in a positive way? She found her own solution: have the book ready, choose a book that is easier to understand, spend time introducing vocabulary with props to aid comprehension. That was an effective use of data for Jon. ■

- **Results of children's assessments.** These may be observational tools or standardized assessments that give a score or have a scale. Both types of assessments complement each other and are necessary to have a comprehensive picture of children's growth and learning. Together, you and the teacher might look at the results and rejoice in the good progress the children are making, or you could make plans for changing instruction so they learn more.

Using all the data you have at your disposal, you are bound to have rich conversations with teachers about children's development, learning, and behavior, and you will create many opportunities to solve problems together. You are putting your heads together toward a common agenda. You are moving in the same direction. Through these rich interactions, you will have built a productive professional relationship with teachers, even if a friendship never develops.

Put Yourself in the Mind of the Teacher

In addition to using data, you can nurture your professional relationship with teachers by anticipating their needs, by putting yourself in the mind of the teacher. You are likely familiar with this concept through any past work as a teacher or with teachers. Effective teachers constantly put themselves in the minds of their learners. Before being with the children, they have to plan. What skill or knowledge do children need to learn? What is somewhat important, what is important, what is absolutely essential? Once with the students, teachers implement activities and continually make adjustments. How are students reacting? At the end of the day or the lesson, the reflection is also about the children. What happened? Were the learning objectives met?

The same ideas apply to the job of leaders who support teachers. After classroom observations and during meetings and conversations with teachers, leaders should ask themselves: How are teachers reacting? What is keeping them engaged? How can I modify my actions and behaviors to make the participation and contribution of teachers more meaningful and rich? Are the goals of our organization met with the current situation? Are the goals of teachers being met? Putting yourself in the minds of your teachers is very difficult work. It is knowledge work and relationship work. It is thinking and feeling. Teaching is called relationship-based work. Leading is also relationship-based work. As you anticipate and meet teachers' needs, you build trust, nurture the relationship, and help teachers feel supported in their profession.

ENCOURAGING A CULTURE OF COLLABORATION

A caring community of workers is not just about positive relationships between leaders and teachers. It is also about relationships among teachers. Education leaders are responsible for facilitating these relationships, much in the same way teachers are responsible for facilitating collaboration among children.

MONIQUE, *Education Coordinator and Coach*
Monique has a strategy to help foster collaboration. She teams up experienced teachers with new teachers, creating a "buddy system." This practice promotes many opportunities for teachers to interact, whether to find materials in the resource room or to share ideas about teaching. ■

Another technique for encouraging collaboration is using team-building exercises. I am not suggesting time-consuming games. I recommend exercises that focus on professional interests and skills. This kind of activity helps individuals acknowledge one another's expertise. It promotes professional respect and a sense of community. These activities are best done as short warm-ups before formal meetings. Here is an example of a team-building activity modeled after the "Think, Pair, Share" activity we do with children:

1. Pose a question to the group, such as, "What is one fun and educational early literacy activity you have done in the last two weeks?" Allow teachers a few minutes to think about the question on their own.

2. Have teachers pair up and discuss the question together.

3. Ask pairs to share their answers with the whole group

You can promote a culture of collaboration in many ways; the key is to get teachers working together.

COMMUNICATING EFFECTIVELY

"People problems" are often communication problems. One person interprets another person's message through her own lens, which may not translate to the intended or full meaning. Misunderstandings or misinterpretations may result, which can cause hurt feelings and strain relationships. Communication is always a two-way process. Someone communicates something and the other person receives the message. The speaker's intention and the listener's interpretation have to match.

We communicate in many ways. We communicate verbally and in writing. We also communicate with our body language. Regardless of personality, education leaders have to communicate carefully to build trust and foster a caring community.

Make Expectations Clear

Teachers need to know what their leaders expect from them. Assumptions can be dangerous. What you assume teachers know may be very different from what they actually think or believe or understand.

> **JON,** *Principal*
>
> Jon bought a new curriculum for the kindergarten classrooms. It was expensive, and he expected it to be a valuable tool for the teachers. He provided training on it and expressed his hopes that the teachers would use it with enthusiasm. When they did not, he became frustrated and secretly blamed them for not being committed to their profession. Why else would they ignore his efforts and the expense?
>
> After thinking about it, Jon realized that he had expressed his "hopes" about the curriculum rather than clearly stating his expectations for its use. When he stated his expectations more directly, the situation changed in a good way. ■

Here is the difference between stating expectations unclearly and clearly:

- **Unclear expectation:** "This curriculum is part of the district's new plan. It is very expensive and has gotten good reviews. I hope it will be useful to you. I know it will be good for the kids. Let me know how it goes."

- **Clear expectation:** "This curriculum is part of the district's new plan. It is very expensive and has gotten good reviews. I hope it will be useful to you. I know it will be good for the kids. Now that training is over, we have to implement it. Using this curriculum is not a choice. The first phase needs to happen within three months. I will come every two weeks to observe how it works in your classroom. We'll meet and discuss how it's going. There may be some adjustments to make. I'll support you in the implementation. We'll figure it out together."

Do you see the difference in tone as well as in words? With clear expectations, the goals of the leader are transparent—there is no hidden agenda. The message is a little longer but it is direct and clear.

Find Many Ways to Communicate, and Communicate Often

Successful organizations use multiple ways to communicate. Communication needs to happen officially in large groups, small groups, and individually. It needs to happen in writing and in person. When communication is not explicit, a secondary system of rumors and hearsay tends to develop through the grapevine. Sometimes this type of information is spread through "parking lot meetings," gatherings outside of the building where teachers gossip or exchange their fears. As in the old-fashioned telephone game, wild ideas can be generated and spread this way, causing anxiety and bad feelings. This undermines or prevents a caring community. If you are not clearly communicating information to your teachers, they will fill in the blanks with their own ideas and interpretations. Here is a straightforward system of communication I encourage you to try:

- **Communicate verbally in large-group and small-group meetings** (every two weeks, for thirty to forty-five minutes). A big part of your communication plan should be establishing regular face-to-face group meetings. Regular meetings are important ways to share information and to take a planned break from the busyness of the classroom. These official gatherings are worth the investment of time and money for the opportunities they provide to share information and communicate changes. They are also a good time to discuss challenges, come up with solutions, and collaborate on projects. Based on the size of your staff and the number of classrooms, you might consider a meeting at the classroom level every two weeks, and a large-group staff meeting once a month.

- **Communicate verbally *and* in writing for official purposes, such as sharing policies or new directives** (as often as you have news to share). Both forms of communication should be used for the same message, to reinforce its importance.

- **Communicate in writing to the group** (twice a month). Bi-monthly e-mails or handouts on program or school happenings will keep everyone in the loop.

- **Communicate verbally with individuals** (daily). This is likely to happen daily in informal ways. You should make a point of connecting in person with every teacher, even by just popping into the classroom to say hello. More formal one-on-one short meetings to check in are also a good way to keep communication open.

- **Communicate in writing to individuals** (weekly). Communicating regularly with individuals is a helpful way to check in and follow up on specific issues that do not relate to the larger group. On the next page you will find a weekly communication form that can be completed on paper or by e-mail. You will find a reproducible version of this form in the appendix.

Weekly Communication Form

To: _____ Date: _____

From: _____ Site: _____

Recognition or something that was meaningful for me this week:

Concerns and recommendations:

Things I would like you to know:

I need your assistance in:

With e-mail, texting, and various social media tools, there is some confusion about the most appropriate ways to communicate in a work environment. Decide what tools you will use, and be consistent in delivery. E-mail has its place for giving affirmations that do not require a conversation, as you might write a thank-you or greeting card to someone, but e-mail (and texting) should not be used for bringing up concerns. The telegraphic style does not give enough context, and it is easy to misunderstand the message. E-mail is not a tool for feedback.

To respect professional boundaries, it is best if you do not become friends with teachers on Facebook or other social media sites.

Listen as Well as Speak

Speaking and listening are the dance of communication. Listening may be the most difficult part because it requires silence, but silencing our own thoughts helps us pay attention to the words of the other person. What is the person saying that is meaningful to the situation?

> ### SARA, *Center Director*
> Sara and teacher Mary were having a discussion about lunchtime. Teacher Mary was frustrated about the four-year-olds' new habit of banging their spoons on the table at the beginning of the meal. When one started, there was a chain reaction. Along with the laughing, the noise was deafening and the scene seemed out of control. Teacher Mary blamed the children for the behavior and an "obnoxious little boy" for starting it. She wanted Sara to talk to his parents immediately. As teacher Mary talked, Sara wanted to help quickly and started to give solutions. She stopped talking when she noticed that teacher Mary only had "yes, but" responses. Sara went silent and she listened, which seemed awkward at first. Teacher Mary continued ranting for a while, but eventually slowed down. As she slowed down, she came up with two solutions to fix the mealtime problem on her own: wait until the meal was ready to ask the children to sit down, and give the boy the task to distribute the napkins. In the end, listening was productive. It helped teacher Mary reflect and problem solve on her own. ■

In addition to frustrations and challenges in the classroom, teachers must have opportunities to express their worries and have those worries heard by their leaders. As you listen to worries, ask yourself, what does this teacher need from me? Unless you listen attentively, you won't know whether the teacher simply needs encouragement or a more intensive form of support.

JON, *Principal*

Teacher Julie will have ten children who are English-language learners this year. The apartment complex across the street from the school has become a relocation center for refugees. This is a new situation for Julie, and she is very worried about doing a good job, but she is not sure how to bring it up for fear of appearing insecure. The fact is, even though she has been teaching for ten years, this situation will require different techniques. Jon, her principal, meets with her before the school year starts to see how she is feeling. He listens to her concerns. He agrees about the new challenges, and together they make a plan for materials and training. In addition, Jon decides to visit Julie's classroom once a week to observe and check in on her. Julie feels relieved that she does not have to figure out the challenge on her own. ■

Leaders do not have to know everything, and that is a good thing. This attitude liberates leaders to try new things and change their minds based on feedback from their teachers. Teachers may have suggestions for changing policies or practices that benefit everyone. They may also complain or express a worry about issues that you have not thought about. Listening to the ideas that come to you does not mean you have to respond immediately. Many times, waiting before you respond is best. A day or a week may be necessary to give an idea or complaint some thought or to find a solution. As you listen to teachers' ideas, complaints, and worries, be sure to maintain confidentiality and avoid the "so-and-so-said" type of negative communication. Then make sure you get back to the individuals within one or two days to let them know that you are working on their idea. If the idea is not workable, tell them that too, with the reasons.

Welcome Feedback

Communicate clearly that you welcome feedback, and model how to receive it gracefully. Invite teachers to give you feedback in person or in writing. Some teachers may do it well. Others may not have much experience giving feedback, and they may do so clumsily. Leaders who open themselves up for feedback may hear things they don't like. Be brave. It shows that you are part of your community of workers and that feedback isn't something to be feared. At a staff meeting, report on any concerns or the affirmations you have received so everyone can hear them at the same time.

Give Feedback and Offer Solutions Thoughtfully

Providing feedback on teachers' work and ideas is essential and must be done with care. Effective feedback will help you foster your caring community by proving you can be trusted. It also sends the message that you are paying attention. Providing feedback poorly, on the other hand, will break down your caring community—by creating distrust and fear, making teachers question your intentions, and suggesting that you are not caring or empathetic.

The purpose of giving feedback is to help teachers reflect so they can improve their performance. In order for feedback to be effective, leaders must establish a common understanding of the feedback process with teachers. Teachers need to know, for example, that receiving feedback and collaborating on that feedback is an expectation of the job. Leaders have rules to follow too, rules that will encourage the positive result of helping teachers improve their performance:

- **Be direct and nonjudgmental.** You might wonder, how can I not pass judgment when I give feedback to a teacher? The answer is to not pass judgment on the teacher as a person. As a giver of feedback, you simply describe actions in relation to expectations or standards of early childhood education, rather than communicating that the teacher is good or bad. You are comparing actions to the standards and helping the receiver identify how these actions match or do not match the standards. This approach helps teachers reflect on their actions and decide for themselves to make changes to improve.

- **Do not give feedback on the run.** You need to prepare. Feedback should be scheduled and planned in advance, with supporting evidence such as observations or video clips. The giver needs to keep the recipient's personality in mind and to rehearse what to say and how. The space should be quiet and without distraction.

- **Use a friendly tone and invite the recipient to ask questions and for clarifications.** A good strategy is to start the feedback session with affirmations of actions that are going well for that teacher, referring to observed behaviors and actions that are positive. Make it clear to the teacher that she is welcome and encouraged to respond to the feedback.

- **Choose your words carefully.** Your choice of words is critically important. Avoid labels or judging words (*good, bad,* and *mediocre*) and extreme words (*always* and *worst*). Instead use action-focused phrases, such as "When I saw . . .," or "When the children . . ."

- **Show empathy while remaining focused and firm.** The teacher may go off on tangents, in an intentional or unintentional effort to redirect the conversation. Listen and be understanding, but most importantly, return the conversation to the main object.

The ideal result of feedback is for the recipient to find solutions on her own. She will get the insights she needs to experience the "aha" moment and make changes. If this magical moment does not happen spontaneously, the leader is responsible for making explicit the changes that need to be made and for helping the teacher develop a list of steps to improve. The final result of feedback should be a joint agreement on what to do.

MONIQUE, *Education Coordinator and Coach*

On Tuesday, Monique observed a small-group science lesson. After circle time, six preschool children came to their assigned table with Mr. Jenkins. His lesson plan said he was going to teach about ice melting and turning into water. He had ice cubes in a tray and an eyedropper with food coloring. He gave a quick explanation about ice cubes melting in warm air. After that the children were allowed to manipulate the ice cubes for the next ten minutes. They were happy and smiling, but Monique was concerned that they did not learn much from this small-group exercise. She was looking forward to the debriefing the next day. This is how the conversation went:

Monique: Hi, Mr. Jenkins. Thanks for being on time. How has your day been going?

Mr. J.:   Great, thanks. I am a bit tired though. My baby is not sleeping at night.

Monique: Yeah, those babies when they are teething. [*smile*] I want to take a few minutes to debrief on your small-group science lesson yesterday and give you some feedback.

Mr. J.:   Okay. But I have to get back to the classroom in fifteen minutes.

Monique: Yes, we'll be done in fifteen minutes. How did you feel it went yesterday?

Mr. J.:   Great, the kids had a wonderful time.

Monique: Yes, they did. They were laughing and smiling. They loved feeling the ice cubes.

Mr. J.:   Yeah!

Monique: What do you think they learned?

Mr. J.:   [*silence*] Hmm. They learned about melting.

Monique: [*opens the early childhood standards*] What indicators were guiding you?

Mr. J.:   [*browses the list and hesitates*] "Uses scientific inquiry skills"?

Monique: Which ones do you think they practiced the most?

Mr. J.:   Maybe "solves problems"? Frankly, I don't think they did practice it much. They just enjoyed the activity.

Monique: I am thinking having fun is not enough. When we looked at the children's vocabulary scores last week, they were low, remember? What do you think could have helped the children learn more?

Mr. J.:   You know, I have a book I could have read beforehand to help them prepare. It is very simple but explains the process of melting. I could have asked questions too.

cont'd

Monique: Yes, that list of questions we got at the CLASS training, to promote concept development?

Mr. J.: Yes, those would be good.

Monique: Let's take a quick look at these questions. [*They both look at the list of questions and underline some of them.*]

Monique: Almost time to end our conference. Let's make a plan for the next small group, okay? I want to come and observe in two weeks. [*They make a plan together on how Mr. Jenkins will use questions to promote concept development during small-group time.*] ∎

In the example, Monique gives feedback to the situation, not to Mr. Jenkins' specific behavior. In this manner, she helps him see the situation from the outside and he gets to his own conclusion. Sometimes education leaders feel that they have to *be* the truth, when all they have to do is hold up the truth with the tools of the trade at their disposal—such as early learning standards—which I find liberating. In the example, the feedback is not about Monique's opinion, it is about what the science of early childhood education says should be happening. It is about best practices of teaching so children learn best. Both Monique and Mr. Jenkins can rally around this effort.

Give Affirmations

I hear lots of "Good jobs!" echoing through classrooms and hallways when I visit centers and schools. This praising reflex is not a good instructional strategy. We know that children develop more confidence in their abilities when they get *specific* affirmations, rather than empty praise, regardless of how loudly the praise is shouted. The same concept applies to teachers.

Teaching is a fairly lonely job. Teachers do not get comments from their young students about what they are doing, so those of us in the business of supporting teachers have to be intentional about affirming good work. This does not mean a global "good job!" to them, either. Even adding a box of treats on Friday morning will not boost teachers' professional selves. Education leaders need to be a mirror for teachers who cannot see themselves. That will help boost teachers' sense of efficacy.

Praise sounds like this:

- "Hey Peter, good job this morning with the crying toddlers!"

- "Wow, Kathy, that was a great science activity!"

Affirmations sound like this:

- "Peter, I noticed how you organized your team with primary comforters for separation anxiety of the toddlers. Your good planning is working! The room calmed down quickly."

- "Kathy, I saw the children asking big questions about the seeds in the science activity. You were teaching them new vocabulary, and they were very engaged in the lesson."

In the first examples, a harried teacher will hear it and think, "Okay, whatever!" In the second set of examples, an equally harried teacher will hear it and think, "I do have a plan! She noticed. I am a good teacher. All the time I spent planning shows, it is worth it." These teachers are likely to have a bigger smile and lighter step to help them carry the day. They feel supported in their hard work and a part of a caring community.

MODELING CARING AND EMPATHY

Interpersonal conflict is common in centers and schools. Teachers do not get along, or they do not share materials. There may be gossip and hard feelings. These situations are negative and should not happen in your school. They are destructive and contrary to what we teach children. To help with these problems, education leaders have the responsibility to model caring and empathy, to set the tone of a caring community.

MONIQUE, *Education Coordinator and Coach*

Teacher Alicia and her assistant, Becky, are not speaking to each other. Becky feels that Alicia does not respect her experience and dismisses her ideas. They both complain about each other to Monique. Monique is irritated, but she listens. She does not report to either one what the other has said. She does ask them individually if they are willing to have her facilitate a meeting to clarify their concerns. They agree. During the meeting, Monique helps Alicia and Becky repair their relationship by pointing out how they themselves help children get along. They end up chuckling that they had acted like two four-year-olds. Monique was patient and compassionate in her approach. She did not judge the teachers; she worked to build a caring community. ■

MAINTAINING YOUR CARING COMMUNITY OF WORKERS

Maintaining a positive and caring work environment is not a one-time event. It is a continuous process. You must be diligent in nurturing positive relationships every day, consistently reinforcing and supporting joint goals, and tending to your lines of communication to keep them clear and open. Maintaining your caring community can be a challenge, especially when conflicts erupt. When we work with adults, we feel like they should always act like the grown-ups they are! Leaders are disappointed when there is conflict and confusion in work teams. They worry that these adults are just acting childish. I understand the sentiment.

I also believe it is the job of leaders to create and maintain morale. As we expect teachers to do with children, leaders must nurture a nonjudgmental attitude and help teachers feel accepted. Your efforts to create and maintain a caring environment for your workers will help teachers feel supported and secure in giving and receiving feedback. All of this will pave the way for a positive and effective teacher evaluation process.

Reflection Questions _____

1. Teaching and managing are "people businesses." What does this statement mean to you?

2. Review the strategies and tools for creating a caring community of workers. Which ones are you already using? Which ones are you not using? Choose one idea and commit to using it for a month. Reflect on the results.

3 RECOGNIZING TEACHER QUALITY

We simply cannot be content with the inequities in early experience that contribute to school failure and lifelong negative consequences for so many of our nation's children.

—Carol Copple and Sue Bredekamp, *Developmentally Appropriate Practice in Early Childhood Programs Serving Children from Birth through Age 8*

Children in early childhood education programs do not all have the same quality experiences. Some centers and schools are very good. Others are not. The difference is in teaching quality. Teaching quality determines the quality of a program and directly impacts student learning (Copple and Bredekamp 2009; Stronge 2007). Children who receive high-quality teaching learn more (Schmoker 2006). Children who receive poor-quality teaching learn less, and the effect is cumulative. They continue to lose academic ground the longer they stay with a bad teacher (Sanders and Rivers 1996). The reality is that there are good teachers and there are bad teachers, and children's education is affected accordingly (Reagan, Case, and Brubacher 2000).

Improving teaching quality must be a priority for all education leaders who want to improve children's education. Doing so *requires* teacher evaluation. Common sense, observation, and research tell us that education and experience are not enough to ensure quality of teaching (Burchinal, Hyson, and Zaslow 2011). Teachers with higher levels of education may have more knowledge, but they are not necessarily better teachers. Neither are teachers with many years of experience. I see evidence of this in centers and schools everywhere.

Just as teachers must evaluate children's learning and development regularly in order to provide the instruction and scaffolding necessary for improvements, so too must education leaders evaluate teachers. Only through evaluations will leaders—and teachers—be able to review and quantify teaching quality. Only through evaluations will leaders know how best to foster professional growth (and know whether growth is happening over time). And all teachers—even good ones—need and benefit from ongoing feedback on their performance.

In many programs, teachers are assessed only once a year through an observation of the classroom followed by an annual performance review instead of receiving the regular evaluations and feedback they need to improve. Goals are written and often forgotten until the following year. This is not good enough for teachers and the children they serve. As education leaders, we need to take responsibility for quality improvement at our settings and make improvement happen through ongoing evaluations of teachers followed by support.

In spite of the benefits of evaluation, education leaders and teachers alike carry many reservations about assessing teachers' skills and practices. Teachers and teachers' unions want guarantees that evaluation will not penalize teachers unfairly and arbitrarily. They worry about simplistic methods of evaluation, such as using only student test scores to decide if a teacher is good or not. I agree that measuring quality using only one source of data is insufficient, but these concerns shouldn't prevent evaluations from happening altogether. Instead, we need a comprehensive way to evaluate teachers that goes beyond "just the test scores," but also beyond "just a quick annual observation" (Tucker and Stronge 2005; Schmoker 2006).

As we begin to strategize for a system of evaluating teaching quality, we first have to determine *what* quality teaching is. Fortunately, concepts of quality teaching are not mysterious in our field; we already have many resources that define quality. Unfortunately, the information in these resources tends to be dense and many of them address only part of a teacher's job or only some of the aspects important to teaching quality. For example, the Quality Rating and Improvement Systems (QRISs) typically measure quality through teacher qualifications, class size, and adult–child ratios within a program, but they usually do not measure teacher-child interactions, teaching skills, or children's learning outcomes—which are essential elements of teaching quality. And even though QRISs promote using assessments to measure children's learning, they do not offer guidance on how leaders should use the results of these assessments as indicators of teaching quality (Zellman and Karoly 2012). Recent QRIS evaluations are beginning to demonstrate that these aspects of teaching quality should be added to solidify the credibility of the QRIS (Sabol et al. 2013). These additions seem intuitively obvious and urgent. Ignoring aspects of teacher quality should not be an option (Pianta 2011; Kagan and Gomez 2011; Goffin 2013).

In this chapter, I will help you navigate through the numerous resources available for defining and recognizing quality in teaching. There are many and they are very good, even those that have limited focus. As education leaders, we simply need the will and the discipline to organize the content in our minds and in our assessment tools so we can comprehensively *measure* that quality in our settings. I will help you in this effort by proposing a simple model for viewing the teacher's job so you have a framework for your evaluations. But first, let's consider the three aspects of teaching that compose quality.

IDENTIFYING THREE ASPECTS OF QUALITY TEACHING

Teacher A has excellent rapport with children and good classroom management skills. She provides interesting and fun learning activities, but she organizes these activities based on her own interests more than on what the children need to learn. When asked how she knows what the children are learning, she answers, "I can just see they are doing well." She believes the parents do not care about education because few attend parent-teacher conferences. She gets along well with colleagues and is always ready to share materials and ideas.

Teacher B has nice rapport with the children and good classroom management skills. She provides interesting and fun learning activities based on the curriculum adopted by the program. She is often absent, but she does a fine job when she is there. Her coworkers are often irritated by her erratic attendance.

Teacher C has nice rapport with the children and good classroom management skills. She assesses children three times a year. She shares the information with her teaching assistant, and they use data to plan the learning activities. She modifies the curriculum adopted by her program to fit the needs of her students. She sends a weekly e-mail to families to let them know what the children are working on. Attendance at parent-teacher conferences is high. She does not get along with her colleagues. She complains that staff meetings are a waste of time.

If we were to evaluate these three teachers using only a one-time classroom observation, we would see that they have nice classrooms with mostly happy children roaming about. We would miss weaknesses in other crucial professional responsibilities that affect children's learning. We wouldn't see, for example, that the children in Teacher A's class were not meeting learning standards for their age because essential subject matter wasn't being taught or taught thoroughly. We wouldn't consider Teacher B's absences and how the lack of consistent instruction by a consistent educator was reducing quality experiences for the children. And we wouldn't think about how Teacher C's lack of collegiality limits her growth and the growth of less experienced teachers she could mentor.

A good evaluation model, then, needs to address the three fundamental aspects of a teacher's job:

1. acts of teaching (what the teacher does directly with the children in the classroom);

2. results of teaching (what children learn as the result of the acts of teaching); and

3. professional behaviors (behaviors that make a teacher a good worker).

Quality in all areas indicates true quality of teaching.

Acts of Teaching

Acts of teaching are the technical components of instruction and classroom management. They include skills such as implementing a curriculum, planning lessons, and designing activities for all areas of development. For example, teachers use various strategies to teach reading, math, social studies, art, and social skills. These are acts of teaching. Teachers' efforts to create a positive emotional climate and a learning-friendly physical environment are also acts of teaching. Teachers must expect and reinforce positive behavior and help children deal with conflict. They must organize their physical space and select and supply materials that are engaging, thoughtfully prepared, and intentionally organized so children can be active and productive in the classroom.

Acts of teaching are typically evaluated through classroom observations, sometimes using tools such as formal validated assessments and less-formal checklists or evaluation forms created by a center or school. Strengths and weaknesses in acts of teaching might also be revealed through measured results of teaching (data about what children are learning), but this data about children's learning is only a piece of a larger puzzle and should not alone determine the quality of acts of teaching.

SARA, *Center Director*
Sara was concerned about what was happening in infant classroom A. The babies' individual schedules were followed and the health practices were good. But the lead teacher was so concerned about safety that when the babies were awake, she kept each baby strapped in a baby bouncer. She allowed fifteen minutes of floor time for only three babies at a time. This was unacceptable. Sara made a plan to talk to the teacher about developmentally appropriate practice for infants, give her information, and improve the acts of teaching in this classroom. ■

Results of Teaching

The ultimate results of teaching are children's learning. How much do the children know after they have received instruction? How are they progressing in their academic and cognitive skills? Results of teaching also include how children behave in the classroom. Social-emotional skills are as important as academic skills, and they are learned with the guidance of teachers.

Teachers must know about and use appropriate assessments to measure children's learning in all areas of development. They have to be competent using a combination of authentic observational and standardized tools. Teachers also need to know how to examine children's work and behavior over time to assess progress. They have to analyze the results to teach intentionally; they need to use the data to tailor teaching to the children's needs. Finally, they must have a system to share the data with coworkers and families (McAfee, Leong, and Bodrova 2004).

Results of teaching are typically measured through observational assessments, standardized tests, and portfolios of children's work, all of which are usually conducted or prepared by the teachers. All evaluations of results of teaching should be developmentally and culturally appropriate, valid, and reliable. Teachers or other staff members administering the assessments must be trained in the protocols of the tests. State QRISs have lists of approved tools on their websites. I encourage you to check with your state's requirements. This information is readily available online.

JON, *Principal*

In one third-grade classroom, children's scores are consistently low in math. In another third-grade classroom, they are consistently high. After close examination of the data and discussions with teachers, Jon finds out that the teacher with the low scores "just does not like math." It is not that the children are not good at math, it is that they are not taught math. Jon makes a plan to show the teacher the cause and effect relationship between teaching and learning. ■

Professional Behaviors

Professional behaviors are those expected in any job, in any field. They relate to reliability and attendance, personal appearance, relationships with colleagues and clients, and general demeanor. Professional behaviors important for early childhood professionals include appropriate dress and personal grooming, being on time, maintaining confidentiality, being courteous and friendly, being reliable and cooperative, and demonstrating a positive attitude in actions and in conversations with colleagues, children, and parents.

Professional behaviors are often the most difficult for education leaders to address because they are of such a personal nature. Education leaders are afraid to become too involved in the teacher's personal life, or they just hope the issues will go away. Out of generosity, they sometimes wait too long to deal with problems of attendance, dress, or poor interpersonal skills.

Professional behaviors are observed informally throughout the day. Strengths in this area are typically ignored and weaknesses are evaluated when they interfere with good functioning such as frequent absenteeism or texting in class.

MONIQUE, *Education Coordinator and Coach*

Monique had to address the delicate situation of teacher Cassie whose clothes were flashy and revealing. They were appropriate for a nightclub outing but not for teaching preschoolers. Monique could no longer ignore the issue when colleagues and parents started rolling their eyes. Fortunately the program had a statement about personal appearance and dress in the personnel policy handbook. In the privacy of Monique's office, they discussed the concern and the educational reasons for it. They then made a plan. ■

REVIEWING THE LITERATURE ON TEACHING QUALITY

The field of early childhood education has excellent resources to guide our thinking about all three aspects of quality. These resources are the philosophical foundation of early childhood education, and you are likely familiar with many of them. They describe and define what education leaders and teachers know or should know about teaching and learning. As you read, think about how the definitions and standards relate to the daily job of your teachers. Take note of any passages, standards, or definitions that match the priorities of your setting or that support your goals for children and teachers. Start to use the language and the ideas from these resources when you give teachers feedback on their skills. Make teaching quality a common topic of discussion at your setting, even before evaluations take place.

Resources on Quality Acts of Teaching

Numerous resources exist to help you recognize and define quality acts of teaching. Take time to acquire and read through the publications you are unfamiliar with and to review the ones you are already well versed in. Know that some of these resources also address—to various extents—the other two aspects of teaching quality, results of teaching and professional behaviors. Even so, in efforts to understand quality acts of teaching, I consider these to be the primary guides.

Teacher Definitions from NAEYC:
Guidelines for Developmentally Appropriate Practice

The National Association for the Education of Young Children (NAEYC) has developed guidelines for being an excellent teacher of children ages birth to eight, which can be found in their position statement on developmentally appropriate practice (NAEYC 2009) and in the book *Developmentally Appropriate Practice in Early Childhood Programs Serving Children from Birth through Age 8* (Copple and Bredekamp 2009). According to these resources, being an excellent teacher means

- creating a caring community of learners;
- using a wide range of teaching strategies to enhance development and learning;
- planning the curriculum with goals in mind;
- assessing children's learning; and
- having reciprocal relationships with families.

The themes of quality acts of teaching described in the guidelines are the same as those for education in the upper grades: sound instruction that is a balance of teacher-guided and student-guided activities; curriculum activities that are tailored to the development of children and what they need to learn; classroom management that is consistent and humane; and good relationships with children, parents, and other colleagues.

Early Childhood Generalist Standards

The professional standards for early childhood educators from the National Board for Professional Teaching Standards (NBPTS) give similar guidance to understanding quality acts of teaching. You can find these standards in the third edition of *Early Childhood Generalist Standards* (NBPTS 2012), available at www.nbpts.org. According to this resource, accomplished early childhood teachers of children ages three to eight

- use their knowledge of child development to understand young children and foster each child's development and learning;

- work with families and community partners to support children's growth and to advocate for young children;

- understand and embrace diversity, acting with equity and fairness;

- integrate the basics of the subjects they teach and understand how children think about these ideas in order to support learning;

- organize and manage the learning environment to promote learning;

- follow early childhood objectives and set goals for the group of children as well as for individual children;

- provide instruction that is developmentally appropriate;

- assess children's learning with developmentally appropriate tools;

- reflect on how children are learning and make adjustments to their teaching accordingly; and

- are leaders, collaborators, and advocates for young children and their profession.

The NAEYC Code of Ethical Conduct

In addition to professional standards, there are ethical standards for quality acts of teaching, found in the *NAEYC Code of Ethical Conduct and Statement of Commitment* (NAEYC 2011b). You can access this document at www.naeyc.org. These standards were developed by NAEYC to offer "guidelines for responsible behavior and set forth a common basis for resolving the principal ethical dilemmas encountered in the field of early childhood education" (2011b, 1). This code can be a practical and empowering resource for both leaders and teachers.

As an example, last December, I introduced the code of ethics to a class of Latina providers taking the Minnesota Child Care Credential (MNCCC) courses in Spanish. The students began to use the code to solve everyday problems and to explain their actions to their leaders. When the manager of one of the centers refused to allow children's books to be placed on low shelves, for fear the children would destroy them, two of the teachers looked up the relationship of the manager's directive to the ethical standards. They found the answer in section

I-1.2, which directs teachers "to base program practices upon current knowledge and research in the field of early childhood education, child development, and related disciplines, as well as on particular knowledge of each child." They coupled this ideal with the research they had learned in class about early literacy and the necessity for children to have books available at all times. They presented their findings to the manager and persuaded him to change his mind. It was an easy task since all the center advertising claims the use of best practices. Now the children have access to books.

Core Competencies for Early Childhood Educators

Many states have developed core competencies for early childhood educators of children ages birth to eight. They describe quality acts of teaching based on a teacher's level of education and experience, which are categorized from beginning to advanced. The competencies are divided into content areas, such as child development, curriculum, assessment, families and community, health, program planning and evaluation, and professional development and leadership. If your state does not have such a document, you may view examples from Washington state at www.del.wa.gov/publications/partnerships/docs/CoreCompetencies.pdf or from Minnesota at http://www.mncpd.org/docs/cc_early_childhood.pdf.

The core competencies are designed as a guide, but are often "worded so they can be measured or demonstrated" (MnAEYC 2004, 2), which means they can be used as criteria on an evaluation tool.

Books on Developmentally Appropriate Practice from NAEYC

NAEYC has many excellent resources on developmentally appropriate practices that will help you recognize quality acts of teaching. I recommend three books that richly focus on the acts of teaching:

- *Developmentally Appropriate Practice in Early Childhood Programs Serving Children from Birth through Age 8* by Carol Copple and Sue Bredekamp. This book makes clear the importance of excellent teaching. It describes children's development and provides specific examples of what teachers should do and what they should not do. A CD of additional articles and videos reinforces the ideas of the book.

- *Powerful Interactions: How to Connect with Children to Extend Their Learning* by Amy Laura Dombro, Judy Jablon, and Charlotte Stetson. This book describes and demonstrates what teachers need to do to teach well: be present, connect, and extend learning. It is full of examples, dialogues, and reflection exercises for teachers to reflect on their teaching and to improve their practice.

- *The Intentional Teacher: Choosing the Best Strategies for Young Children's Learning* by Ann S. Epstein. This book reinforces the concept that both children and teachers are active participants of the learning process. It focuses on the balance of child-guided and teacher-guided experiences.

Validated Assessments of Quality Acts of Teaching

In addition to the resources that provide guidelines, standards, and definitions of quality acts of teaching, the criteria from validated assessments are also helpful for recognizing quality acts of teaching. The assessments can, of course, be used as evaluation tools in their own right; the scores and the rubrics will provide objective data to education leaders on quality acts of teaching and give objective feedback to teachers about their work. Three tools are widely used to measure quality acts of teaching in the classroom:

- **Classroom Assessment Scoring System (CLASS).** The Classroom Assessment Scoring System (CLASS), developed at the University of Virginia, focuses on the interactions between teachers and children and has a strong literacy and language focus. This assessment tells us that quality acts of teaching include positive emotional support, good classroom organization, and strong instructional support for children. The CLASS is an observation tool best implemented by evaluators trained by CLASS experts. Evaluators visit the classroom for a period of three hours. They observe in twenty-minute increments and score according to a strict rubric. You can become certified to conduct the CLASS. Certification is valid for one year and needs to be renewed yearly with a fee, after passing a recertification test. More information can be found at www.teachstone.com.

- **Early Language and Literacy Classroom Observation (ELLCO).** The ELLCO is an observation tool that focuses on early literacy. The *ELLCO Pre-K Tool* and the *ELLCO K–3 Tool* (available from Brookes Publishing at www.brookespublishing.com) measure the quality and frequency of early language and literacy in the classroom. The five sections are classroom structure, curriculum, language environment, books and reading, and print and writing. The evaluator gathers evidence from observation and teacher interviews.

- **Early Childhood Environment Rating Scale (ECERS-R) and the Infant-Toddler Environment Rating Scale (ITERS-R).** The ECERS-R and ITERS-R are tools for observing the whole classroom. Each is organized into seven subscales for space and furnishings, personal care routines, language-reasoning, activities, interaction, program structure, and parents and staff. More information at http://ers.fpg.unc.edu/.

Resources on Quality Results of Teaching

The resources that define what children should know and how they should behave are also plentiful. The resources described below provide good definitions of quality results of teaching.

Early Learning Standards for Children

Every state has developed learning standards for children from birth to eight, as well as for the older grades in education. They are based on research and written with care by experts, following a solid developmental perspective. There may be some slight variation in language and format, but the general content is the same. These standards are the main guide for teachers to understand what children need to learn. Some of the documents explicitly include examples of how teachers can teach the skills children need to learn. You can find the early learning standards for your state by going to the website of the department of education and the department of human services.

Common Core State Standards

Forty-eight states, the District of Columbia, and the Department of Defense have adopted the Common Core State Standards in English language arts and literacy and mathematics. These standards are aligned by grade, starting in kindergarten. Educators are expected to teach content as well as analytical thinking, problem solving, and critical-thinking skills. The Common Core State Standards provides a common language and suggested strategies for teaching and assessing children (Porter et al. 2011). You can find information at www.commoncoreworks.org or www.corestandards.org.

When teachers understand the value of standards and use them as learning goals, they become intentional in their practice (Ritchie and Gutmann 2014). They adapt instruction and scaffold it to the needs of children. Intentional teachers are good teachers.

Standardized Assessments and Observational Assessments

Criteria on standardized and authentic observational assessments can help you get a picture of quality results of teaching. Instructional assessments need to be comprehensive; they must measure all areas of development. The joint position statement of NAEYC and the National Association of Early Childhood Specialists in State Departments of Education (NAECS/SDE) on Early Childhood Curriculum, Assessment, and Program Evaluation provides clear guidance on what these assessments should include.

Standardized assessment of results of teaching include myIGDIs Literacy+, preLAS 2000, or Peabody Picture Vocabulary Test, Fourth Edition (PPVT-4). Authentic observational assessments may include GOLD (published by Teaching Strategies), COR (published by HighScope), or Work Sampling (published by Pearson Learning). Follow the guidelines of your state QRIS to find the tools approved in your area.

Resources on Quality Professional Behaviors

Resources that define quality professional behaviors in early childhood education are less plentiful than those that define quality acts of teaching and results of teaching. In fact, the topic of professional behaviors is largely absent in the literature about teaching. However, section 3 of the *NAEYC Code of Ethical Conduct and Statement of Commitment* (NAEYC 2011b), "Responsibilities to Co-workers and Responsibilities to Employers," confirms that these issues are critical to the quality of teaching. Professional behaviors may be spelled out in the personnel policies manual of your organization. In that case, this manual should be used as a reference for the professional behaviors evaluation. In addition, I recommend two books: *Winning Ways for Early Childhood Professionals: Being a Professional* and *Winning Ways for Early Childhood Professionals: Becoming a Team Player*, both by Gigi Schwiekert. These books are easy to read and will give you specific suggestions to think about appearance, communication, work ethic, or attitude. These matters can be challenging to discuss when there is a problem. The books provide direct language to deal with practical everyday issues such as tardiness, politeness, dress, tattoos, hygiene, cell phone usage, beverages in the classroom, smoking, and other situations that may feel difficult to talk about.

Summary of Resources

The resources described in the previous sections are full of good information about teaching quality. In practice, they may seem like long and wordy documents that are difficult and time consuming to read. Know that understanding teaching quality is an ongoing process for all education leaders; you can start small in your efforts to recognize quality, setting aside a little time each week or each month to review one of the aspects of quality or one of the resources described.

Below is a summary of what aspects of teaching quality are covered in the resources described earlier. Some of the resources do cover multiple aspects of teaching, and this overlap is represented in the summary. Refer to this table as you continue to explore what quality teaching is and as you start to develop your plan for comprehensively evaluating your teachers.

Three Aspects of Teaching Quality

ACTS OF TEACHING	RESULTS OF TEACHING	PROFESSIONAL BEHAVIORS
Developmentally Appropriate Practice in Early Childhood Programs Serving Children from Birth through Age 8 by Carol Copple and Sue Bredekamp	Core competencies for early childhood educators	*NAEYC Code of Ethical Conduct and Statement of Commitment*
Early Childhood Generalists Standards from NBPTS	Early learning standards for children	Teacher definitions from NAEYC
The Intentional Teacher: Choosing the Best Strategies for Young Children's Learning by Ann S. Epstein	*NAEYC Code of Ethical Conduct and Statement of Commitment*	*Winning Ways for Early Childhood Professionals: Being a Professional* by Gigi Schwiekert
NAEYC Code of Ethical Conduct and Statement of Commitment	Observational assessments (Teaching Strategies GOLD, Work Sampling System, HighScope COR)	*Winning Ways for Early Childhood Professionals: Becoming a Team Player* by Gigi Schwiekert
Powerful Interactions: How to Connect with Children to Extend Their Learning by Amy Laura Dombro, Judy Jablon, and Charlotte Stetson	Standardized assessments (myIGDIs Literacy+, preLAS 2000, or PPVT-4)	
Teacher definitions from NAEYC	Teacher definitions from NAEYC	
Validated assessments (CLASS, ELLCO, ECERS-R)		
Other tools accepted by the QRIS in your state		

TEACHING QUALITY CHECKLISTS

To help you further define all aspects of teaching quality, I have designed checklists that summarize the body of knowledge about quality teaching in each of the three aspects: acts of teaching (see page 53), results of teaching (see page 54), and professional behaviors (see page 55). You will find reproducible versions of these checklists in the appendix. These checklists are short and reflect the essence of quality for early childhood teachers. They are easy to use and are designed to quickly help you and your teachers come to a comprehensive and objective picture of teaching quality. They are intended to generate meaningful discussion and lead to problem solving.

To use the checklists, start by thinking about the aspect of teaching you are evaluating. Then gather evidence of quality in that aspect—that is, examples or proof of quality that you see or hear. Finally, determine the frequency of this evidence of quality—how often you notice these examples are happening.

If you "always" observe the positive behaviors and actions indicated in the checklists, that means that teaching is intentional and quality is present. If the results are "sometimes" or "never," be concerned that the teaching may not be of a consistent quality. Search the resources for quality in that aspect (see table on page 51) to find the rationale or suggestions that will help you improve quality in that area.

◆ ◆ ◆

There is enough information about what to teach and how to teach. And there are enough resources to implement good teaching practices. Now that we know what resources are available for defining quality in all aspects of teaching and what standards of quality exist for teachers to be evaluated against, the next step is to figure out how to use this information to evaluate teachers. The next chapter will describe in detail how to conduct regular evaluations of performance, how to acknowledge quality or growth needs, how to address performance problems, and how to help teachers identify areas for professional development.

Reflection Questions _____

1. Lead a discussion about quality of teaching with your staff: What does quality mean to you? Write the group's ideas on chart paper. Compare their ideas to the ideas in this chapter.

2. Review the teaching quality checklists on pages 53–55. How do they serve your needs as you prepare to evaluate teachers? What adaptations would you make?

Checklist for Assessing Quality of Acts of Teaching

This checklist will help you get a general picture of the acts of teaching. It is a tool for observation and discussion. Review the seven acts of teaching and the evidence of quality for that act of teaching below. Observe your teachers and mark how often teachers show evidence of that quality.

The teacher . . .

	ALWAYS	SOMETIMES	NEVER
1. Has an efficient and rich classroom environment			
• The materials are developmentally appropriate and organized for learning.	☐	☐	☐
• The classroom is uncluttered.	☐	☐	☐
• Children are able to access materials on their own.	☐	☐	☐
2. Manages the classroom effectively			
• The schedule for the classroom is developmentally appropriate with a balance of teacher-directed and child-directed activities.	☐	☐	☐
• Conflicts are rare and easily managed.	☐	☐	☐
3. Has a positive rapport with children			
• Children smile, laugh, talk, listen, ask questions, and help each other.	☐	☐	☐
4. Implements the curriculum as directed by the program or school			
• Schedule, activities, and materials reflect the curriculum in all learning centers (literacy, math, science, blocks, library, sensory, manipulatives, meals, circle, large and small groups).	☐	☐	☐
5. Prepares and writes lesson plans for all children			
• A written lesson plan is posted.	☐	☐	☐
• The activities reflect the lesson plan.	☐	☐	☐
6. Provides developmentally appropriate activities that are content rich			
• Children can do the activities at various levels of proficiency.	☐	☐	☐
• Children listen, talk, read, and write throughout the day.	☐	☐	☐
• Children learn by playing, exploring, and experimenting.	☐	☐	☐
7. Assesses children's learning			
• Assessments are developmentally appropriate.	☐	☐	☐
• Assessments are both observational and standardized tools.	☐	☐	☐
• Collected data reflects children's learning and behaviors (notes, photos, work samples, scores, videos).	☐	☐	☐

Checklist for Assessing Quality of Results of Teaching

This checklist will help you get a general picture of quality in results of teaching. It is a tool for observation and discussion. Review the five results of teaching and the evidence of quality for that result of teaching below. Observe your teachers and mark how often teachers show evidence of that quality.

The teacher . . .	ALWAYS	SOMETIMES	NEVER
1. Uses assessments to plan teaching			
• Collected data is organized in portfolios.	☐	☐	☐
• Data is analyzed.	☐	☐	☐
• Data is used to inform teaching at the group level and at the individual level.	☐	☐	☐
2. Recognizes children's growth and learning			
• Children's growth and learning is quantified.	☐	☐	☐
3. Supports children's learning intentionally			
• Children learn.	☐	☐	☐
• Progress happens.	☐	☐	☐
4. Shares with coworkers			
• Coworkers understand what the children are learning and how to support it.	☐	☐	☐
5. Shares with parents			
• Parents understand what their children are learning and how to support it.	☐	☐	☐

Checklist for Assessing
Quality of Professional Behaviors

This checklist will help you get a general picture of quality professional behaviors. It is a tool for observation and discussion. Review the seven professional behaviors and the evidence of quality for those professional behaviors below. Observe your teachers and mark how often teachers show evidence of that quality.

The teacher . . .	ALWAYS	SOMETIMES	NEVER
1. Maintains safety practices			
• Does not use cell phone while on duty with children.	☐	☐	☐
• Follows all health and safety procedures (hand washing, diaper changing, toy cleaning, and so on).	☐	☐	☐
2. Has regular and reliable attendance			
• Absences are rare.	☐	☐	☐
• Absences are justified.	☐	☐	☐
3. Has positive relationships with parents			
• Parents are satisfied with teacher interactions.	☐	☐	☐
• Disagreements with parents are handled respectfully.	☐	☐	☐
• There are no ongoing conflicts with parents.	☐	☐	☐
4. Has positive relationships with colleagues			
• Colleagues are satisfied with interactions.	☐	☐	☐
• Disagreements with colleagues are handled respectfully.	☐	☐	☐
• There are no ongoing conflicts with colleagues.	☐	☐	☐
5. Maintains good personal appearance			
• Dress, shoes, and nails are appropriate for the job of teaching young children (for example, sitting on floor and small chairs, lifting children, playing outside, messy activities, changing diapers).	☐	☐	☐
6. Maintains confidentiality			
• No gossip is generated about families and children.	☐	☐	☐
• No gossip is generated about colleagues.	☐	☐	☐
• Rules of confidentiality are used to stop others from gossiping.	☐	☐	☐
7. Has positive demeanor			
• Tone is positive.	☐	☐	☐
• Tone and language are respectful during disagreements (for example, no shouting, stomping, or threats).	☐	☐	☐

4 TOOLS *and* TECHNIQUES *for* EVALUATING TEACHERS

So far, we have explored the "why" and the "what" of teacher evaluation. Now I want to address the "how." Many people these days, even those outside of early childhood education, are interested in the "how" of teacher evaluations. Policy makers, economists, and the media—who are well aware of the research linking teaching quality and education quality—periodically remind us that teacher accountability and evaluation processes need to change if we want to improve the state of education. The federal government created urgency around the topic in 2009 with an initiative called Race to the Top, which rewards states for "raising student achievement and coming up with the best plans to accelerate education reform" (US Department of Education 2009, 2). These plans must include creating "great teachers and leaders." Since 2009—because of Race to the Top—several states, with the help of private philanthropy, have been experimenting with teacher evaluation systems in order to improve teaching quality.

As these systems are being developed, many questions are being asked:

- Should the field of education use business models for teacher evaluation?

- Should teacher evaluation be a "stacked ranking" model, where teachers are rated on a bell curve with top performers and poor performers at each end? Or should it be a developmental model that focuses on growth and development of each teacher?

- Should the evaluation be based on children's test scores only? What other factors should be included?

Race to the Top is getting lots of advice from businesses that are experimenting with performance evaluation in their own environments—advice that often lacks proven results in quality improvement. For example, the business sector is finding out that the bell curve is not effective in the long run. It slows down creativity and teamwork as employees worry about their ranking and compete with one another in unproductive ways (Morris 2013).

As education leaders, we know our field the best, and we have to find a good system of evaluation that works for early childhood education and the unique needs of our profession, rather than letting other industries tell us what to do. And while there is probably no perfect one-size-fits-all method to comprehensive and effective teacher evaluation that will work in every setting, common sense and best practices should help us come up with a solid approach. So I'd like to come back to the notion of the parallel process. In early childhood education, we are experts in understanding development and developmental growth. We need to apply the same principles of developmental growth to the adults working with children. In this chapter, and from the perspective of the parallel process, I will show you some tools and techniques to do evaluation well in your setting.

A good place to start our thinking about teacher evaluation is with the *NAEYC Code of Ethical Conduct: Supplement for Early Childhood Program Administrators* (NAEYC 2011a). This document is reassuring, as it confirms the importance of evaluation. Even better, it provides guidance on how to do it. The code includes five ideals that directly address the concept of performance evaluation (NAEYC 2011a, 5):

1. "We shall provide staff members with safe and supportive working conditions that respect human dignity, honor confidences, and permit them to carry out their responsibilities through performance evaluation, written grievance procedures, constructive feedback, and opportunities for continuing professional development and advancement" (P-3.1).

2. "We shall inform staff whose performance does not meet program expectations of areas of concern and, when possible, assist in improving their performance" (P-3.9).

3. "We shall provide guidance, additional professional development, and coaching for staff whose practices are not appropriate. In instances in which a staff member cannot satisfy reasonable expectations for practice, we shall counsel the staff member to pursue a more appropriate position" (P-3.10).

4. "We shall conduct personnel dismissals, when necessary, in accordance with all applicable laws and regulations. We shall inform staff who are dismissed of the reasons for termination. When a dismissal is for cause, justification must be based on evidence of inadequate or

inappropriate behavior that is accurately documented, current, and available for the staff member to review" (P-3.11).

5. "In making personnel evaluations and recommendations, we shall make judgments based on fact and relevant to the interests of children and programs" (P-3.12).

This code of ethical conduct offers a matter-of-fact and compassionate approach to performance evaluation: it must happen and it must be done well. Performance evaluation is done well when several criteria are in place:

- clear expectations,
- positive communication,
- respectful interaction,
- comprehensive data,
- specific examples,
- goal setting,
- support and resources, and
- coaching for success.

Notice how evaluation and support go hand in hand in all of the descriptions.

If your organization does not have tools or a process for regular teacher evaluations already in place, this chapter will help you on both fronts. First, I describe the various tools you might use to gather data and measure quality in your setting. Then, I propose a straightforward step-by-step model for evaluations that is comprehensive and follows best practices. If your organization already has tools and a system for evaluating teachers, consider using some of the ideas that follow to complement or improve upon the tools and system you already have.

EVALUATION TOOLS AND TIMING

Evaluation is not a one-time event; it must happen several times throughout the year. Just as children's learning needs to be assessed regularly so teachers can provide appropriate instruction to nurture children's growth, so too must teachers' skills be assessed.

As a guideline, a primary yearly formal evaluation with at least three follow-up evaluations is sufficient for promoting quality teaching in your center or school. The best timing for the primary evaluation depends on your schedule and the demands on it. You may time formal evaluation with the budget cycle if you want to emphasize the connection of performance to compensation. I recommend you do that as a concrete way to reward teachers.

The frequency of follow-up reviews will depend somewhat on the results of the primary evaluation. It will need to be tailored to each teacher's individual needs. To stay within the boundaries of best practices, follow-up observations of a minimum of thirty minutes and feedback sessions of forty-five to sixty minutes should be done three times a year. A teacher with lower skills and higher needs for support will require more time for feedback sessions and likely more follow-up reviews throughout the year.

Gathering Data for 360-Degree Feedback

To effectively evaluate teaching quality, both in your primary evaluation and your follow-up observations, you need to use tools; that is, you need a way to collect data. You need a way to measure and document teaching quality in a comprehensive and systematic way.

To comprehensively collect data, I recommend using a 360-degree feedback approach. With this approach, education leaders are not the sole data gatherers; teachers gather data too. And in addition to leaders and teachers, data is supplied from other invested adults. In this way, teachers are not just evaluated from the top by the education leader; instead, they are evaluated from a number of sources, including parents, coworkers, and the teachers themselves (Talan and Bloom 2004). Teachers use the same observation tools as the education leader to assess themselves. In addition, children's data is used as evidence for evaluation.

In using this or any approach to gathering data, you will need a range of tools to effectively evaluate teachers throughout the year. You will need tools to gather data yourself. You will need tools to help teachers evaluate themselves and the children. And you will need tools to gather data from other invested adults.

Tools for Leader-Gathered Data

As an education leader, you will likely use a variety of tools to collect data for both your primary evaluation and your follow-up reviews. These are some of the most frequently used.

Standardized Classroom Assessments

In chapter 3, I describe some of the validated tools from which you can choose to assess teaching quality, such as the CLASS and the ELLCO. There are many others. Choose standardized tools based on the goals of your setting. I recommend including at least one high-quality, well-researched, validated assessment as part of the data for your primary evaluation so you can see how teaching quality at your setting stacks up against others in the field. For your first observation, I recommend that you cover all the parts of the tool. For follow-up reviews, you may focus only on the items that need improvement.

Other Teacher Observation Tools

If you do not use a validated assessment, it is still important to have an observation tool to give structure to what you see during classroom observations. Your program or school district may already have an instrument you are required to use. In addition to containing specific criteria, observation tools typically include a space for writing notes. You'll need to take many notes describing what you see during the observation. These notes are the evidence that you will use later to explain what happened and to justify your analysis.

The teaching quality checklists from chapter 3 are examples of observation tools. You might want to adapt them based on the priorities for teaching quality at your center. Review the resources on teaching quality from chapter 3 for guidance on the language and criteria to use in any tools you create yourself.

Videotaping

Videotaping vignettes is a powerful way to show teachers what is happening in their classroom. It may make teachers nervous at first, but I encourage you to persist. In the end, all teachers I've videotaped have found it valuable. For best results, use a small, unobtrusive camera and focus it on children's actions rather than on the teacher. Plan on taping segments of one or two minutes, and tape several segments during the course of the observation. Later it will be easy to choose the few examples that illustrate best what you want the teacher to see. Your goal is to show teachers the effect of the instruction on the children so they understand the cause and effect of their teaching.

MONIQUE, *Education Coordinator and Coach*
Monique videotapes an infant classroom to later show the teacher how she teaches language to babies. She makes five short segments when the teacher is on the rug talking with babies. She picks two vignettes to discuss specific examples with the teacher. ■

Tools for Teacher-Gathered Data

Teachers should be active participants in data gathering for evaluations. They can supply data on their own work from their own perspective, as well as data on children's learning.

Teacher Self-Evaluations

It is important that the teacher uses the same tools for self-evaluation that the education leader uses. These may be any tool your program is already using, for example, the ELLCO, the CLASS, or the ECERS-R. Since these instruments are long and complex, you may choose one or two sections for the teacher to use to asses her own practices; make sure the teacher also scores the results. In addition, I recommend you ask teachers to assess themselves using the teacher quality checklists from chapter 3 (see pages 53–55).

By having teachers evaluate themselves using the same tools you will be using, teachers learn the content of the evaluation tool. By reading the rubric and considering the evidence, teachers engage in self-reflection. This experience makes the discussion during performance review meetings meaningful and rich. It allows a thoughtful exchange of ideas between the education leader and the teacher.

Tools That Measure Children's Learning

Child assessments are necessary to find out how children are learning and how much. They are a mark of quality. Your setting may have reliable and valid assessments that your teachers already use, such as HighScope COR, Work Sampling System, Teaching Strategies GOLD, or others. You may also be using developmentally appropriate standardized tests, such as myIGDIs or PPVT. The results of these assessments (for evidence of quality results of teaching, see chapter 3) need to be part of the formula for your teacher evaluations. Children in early childhood education are learning the foundational skills for later academics. Their teachers are responsible for teaching these skills.

Children's Portfolios

Children's portfolios contain samples of work children have been doing over time. For example, from September to May, a teacher collects periodic examples of children signing their names. Since teaching to write is part of the curriculum, a steady progression in the forming and placement of the letters will show

how much the children are learning. Other examples may include pictures of children's block structures, math problems second graders have worked on, and photographs or videos of toddlers sharing toys.

If you would like teachers to create portfolios of children's work with specific content, make sure to give the teacher ample notice, and request that the teacher bring the portfolios and her analysis to the performance review meeting.

Tools to Gather Data from Other Invested Adults

Your evaluations, teachers' self-reflections, and children's outcomes may not be enough to get the full picture of teaching quality. Teachers function in a context that includes other adults. Children and families, for example, are the customers of child care and education and should have an opportunity to review the teachers' services at least once a year. Coworkers also have frequent contact with one another and may provide valuable data about one another's practices, data a leader may not receive elsewhere. Before you use these tools, I recommend that you present them to your teachers and discuss them. They must understand that these surveys are anonymous and confidential. Explain that you will tabulate the results and prepare a summary.

Family Surveys

If your center does not have a family questionnaire, I propose the family survey I have designed (see page 64). You will find a reproducible version of the survey in the appendix. The survey is aligned with the teacher quality checklists from chapter 3, so if you use these checklists as one of your evaluation tools, the information from the survey will be relevant on the same items. I recommend giving the survey to families on a Friday with a one-week timeframe for returning it. It is best to provide it on paper, with a return envelope that can be sealed for confidentiality.

Coworker Surveys

In addition to requesting feedback from families, you might consider collecting data from coworkers using a coworker survey (see page 65). You will find a reproducible version of the survey in the appendix. A teacher's peers often see professional practices, strengths, and weaknesses a leader might not have access to. Though coworkers are sometimes nervous about rating one another, it is still a best practice. Listen to their concerns during the presentation session to decide if you are ready to proceed or would prefer to wait for the next evaluation cycle.

Family Survey

Dear family member,

As part of our teacher evaluation process, we ask parents for their feedback. All surveys are anonymous. We combine the results before we share them with teachers. Please put the completed survey in the envelope and put it in the Parent Survey box on the main desk. Thank you for your thoughts.

Name of teacher: _____   **Date:** _____

Center/school: _____

My child's teacher . . .	YES	SOMETIMES	NO	I DON'T KNOW
1. Has a clean and organized classroom.	☐	☐	☐	☐
2. Manages children's behavior well.	☐	☐	☐	☐
3. Has good rapport with my child.	☐	☐	☐	☐
4. Explains the curriculum to me.	☐	☐	☐	☐
5. Teaches my child social skills (sharing, politeness, caring, and so on).	☐	☐	☐	☐
6. Teaches my child academic skills (talking, reading, math, writing, and so on).	☐	☐	☐	☐
7. Provides fun and interesting activities to do and play.	☐	☐	☐	☐
8. Assesses my child's progress and tells me about it.	☐	☐	☐	☐
9. Communicates well with me.	☐	☐	☐	☐
10. Is friendly and helpful.	☐	☐	☐	☐
11. Is professional in dress and behavior.	☐	☐	☐	☐

I also want to say . . . (Please write any other comment you have below.)

Coworker Survey

Dear staff member,

As part of our evaluation process we ask coworkers for their feedback. All surveys are anonymous. We combine the results before we share them with teachers. Thank you for your thoughts.

Name of teacher: _____ **Date:** _____

Center/school: _____

My coworker . . .	YES	SOMETIMES	NO	I DON'T KNOW
1. Has a clean and organized classroom.	☐	☐	☐	☐
2. Manages children's behavior well.	☐	☐	☐	☐
3. Has good rapport with children.	☐	☐	☐	☐
4. Explains the curriculum of our center/school.	☐	☐	☐	☐
5. Teaches children social skills (sharing, politeness, caring, and so on).	☐	☐	☐	☐
6. Teaches children academic skills (talking, reading, math, writing, and so on).	☐	☐	☐	☐
7. Provides developmentally appropriate activities.	☐	☐	☐	☐
8. Assesses children's progress and discusses data with coworkers.	☐	☐	☐	☐
9. Communicates well with me.	☐	☐	☐	☐
10. Is friendly and helpful.	☐	☐	☐	☐
11. Is professional in dress and behavior.	☐	☐	☐	☐

I also want to say . . . (Please write any other comment you have below.)

• • •

Evaluation should not be based on opinion or hearsay. To be credible, data must be based on real information about what happens in the classroom, what the children learn, and what the teacher does. This kind of data is gathered with the tools described above.

Once you understand what tools to keep in your evaluation toolkit, you are ready to begin planning your evaluations. Next, I propose an evaluation model I have implemented with success in child care settings and have trained others to use.

A COMPREHENSIVE MODEL FOR TEACHER EVALUATION

You have decided to create an evaluation system for your staff. You know it will benefit the teachers in your center or school and, ultimately, the children they serve, who will get a better education because of it. You know evaluations will help you monitor teaching quality and provide teachers with the support they need to improve their skills. While you may believe in the benefits of an evaluation process for teaching, you may also have many other challenges to think about in your daily work. The hardest part in regularly evaluating teachers may be getting started. You might wonder how you will find the time, what tools to use, how best to engage teachers, how to talk with teachers about the results, and how to make evaluations a productive and positive experience.

The step-by-step model outlined on the following page will help you answer these questions and will also help you be systematic in your approach, making evaluations a part of your routine. The model is based on the concept of 360-degree feedback mentioned in the previous section. Teachers are not just evaluated from the top by the education leader but from a number of sources, including parents, coworkers, and the teachers themselves. The model is also based on the parallel process and the five guiding principles first presented on pages 58–59. When evaluation is done well, it reinforces not only the principle of assessing professional skills and growth, but the other four principles— creating a caring community of workers, enhancing professional competence, providing appropriate direction and resources, and facilitating involvement in the field of early childhood education—as well, because good evaluation and support practices are dependent on one another. Best of all, the model requires only six steps:

1. Clarify your thinking about teacher evaluation.

2. Choose or develop evaluation tools.

3. Conduct the evaluation.

4. Analyze the results.

5. Communicate the results.

6. Conduct follow-up reviews.

For this evaluation process to work well, teachers need to be involved at every phase. So in addition to explaining how to implement each step of your evaluation process below, I describe how to involve your teachers in the steps. Throughout this chapter, I invite you to follow Sara in her work of evaluating teachers for the first time. As you read, think about how her efforts relate to yours.

Step 1: Clarify Your Thinking about Teacher Evaluation

You want to evaluate teachers but are wondering how to begin. Start by taking a few minutes to clarify why you are evaluating teachers in the first place. You may have received a directive from your organization. Challenges at your setting may have nurtured your own interest. You may want to improve your QRIS or ECERS-R ratings, which recommend (or include subscales for) using evaluation tools. Perhaps you do not yet have an evaluation system, or you know the system you have is weak. These are great reasons to begin.

Now think about what you hope to achieve from your efforts of evaluation. If this is your first attempt at evaluation, you may simply hope to improve teaching quality at your center and your QRIS rating in the process. If you have been evaluating teachers for a while, you may have more specific hopes for your efforts, such as improving outcomes for a certain learning domain by better supporting teachers' needs in this area. Whatever your overarching reasons for evaluation and whatever you hope to achieve, keep these in mind to motivate you as you move forward.

SARA, *Center Director*

Sara runs an independent child care center that does not have an evaluation system. However, after taking the ECERS-R and looking into the NAEYC accreditation guidelines, she found she needed to have one. To be a good quality program and obtain high scores a center must provide at least one formal written evaluation annually. Other indicators of quality include conducting frequent observations (another form of evaluation), providing supportive feedback to teachers, implementing teacher self-evaluations, addressing teachers' strengths and areas needing improvement, and taking actions to implement the results of the evaluation.

With these guidelines in mind, Sara gives herself six months from announcing the evaluation process to teachers to finishing her first set of formal written evaluations and discussions with teachers. She decides to start with the six lead teachers. ■

Once you have decided to implement evaluations at your setting and have clarified your thinking about them, it's time to communicate your intentions to your teachers. Doing so gives teachers the chance to provide feedback and to express their own hopes and worries about the process. It gives you a chance to address any concerns. By communicating your plan upfront, you build trust with teachers and help maintain rather than disrupt your caring community of workers (see chapter 2).

SARA, *Center Director*

Sara announces at the monthly staff meeting in January that she is putting in place an evaluation system to be implemented by June. Sara explains that to obtain accreditation, the center needs to have a good system for teacher evaluation, which does not exist yet. She asks for feedback on her timeline. Some teachers say they would like it to be shorter, closer to four months, to which she agrees. One teacher asks what the consequences of evaluation might be for their jobs. Sara explains that evaluations aren't meant to make them fear for their jobs; rather, they are meant to support their growth. She mentions that just as teachers must assess children so they can be intentional in their instruction and support of children's learning, so too must she evaluate teachers. Sara tells them her goal is to be intentional in supporting them, and evaluations will help with that effort. ■

Step 2: Choose or Develop Tools for Gathering Data

Once you have clarified your thinking and intentions for evaluation, it's time to figure out what tools you will use to measure teaching quality. Your center or school may already have performance evaluation tools and standards you are required to use. If not, you may need to develop tools from scratch or make decisions about which validated assessments to utilize. Use the descriptions of evaluation tools earlier in the chapter to guide you in selecting appropriate tools for your setting.

Make sure the tools for your primary evaluation allow for 360-degree feedback; that is, gather data yourself, from the teacher, and from other invested adults. And make sure the content of your evaluation tools adequately assesses the three aspects of teaching quality introduced in chapter 3: acts of teaching, results of teaching, and professional behaviors. The teaching quality checklists on pages 53–55 are a summary of what each aspect entails.

SARA, *Center Director*

Sara decides to use both the ELLCO and the teacher performance checklists from chapter 3 for her first evaluations. She selects the ELLCO because it is validated and she wants some hard data to share with one of her funders. She chooses the teacher performance checklists because they relate to the daily requirements of her center. She also adapts the family surveys and coworker surveys to fit the language of her center. ∎

Once you have selected the evaluation criteria and tools, communicate your decisions to the teachers. Teacher evaluation is not a "gotcha" exercise. Teachers must know what they will be evaluated on. They should be familiar with all standards and expectations of the field and those of your center or school, including your expectations for the act of teaching, results of teaching, and professional behaviors.

SARA, *Center Director*

At the next information meeting about the evaluation, Sara gives the teachers copies of the teaching quality checklists to read and discuss. They ask questions and for clarification. They agree the checklists describe their work.

Sara tells the teachers she will be evaluating them using the criteria checklists and they will have an opportunity to assess themselves using this same tool. She mentions she will also be gathering data from three other sources: family surveys, coworker surveys, and children's learning outcomes. Coworkers are defined as the teacher aides and fellow lead teachers. She tells the teachers that data about children's learning outcomes will come from the teachers' own assessments of children's learning.

For the formal classroom observation, Sara tells teachers she will use the ELLCO since the center is focusing on early literacy. Sara shows them all the tools she will use to gather data about their practices. ∎

Step 3: Conduct the Evaluation

To conduct the evaluation, you will need to gather data from all sources using the tools you chose and communicated to teachers in the previous step. The classroom observation requires special attention.

The Classroom Observation

While the teacher needs to know that you will observe her classroom, the time and day should not be fixed. This allows you to have flexibility in your schedule. It also makes the point that the teacher does not need to prepare a special show for your benefit. You are observing just a regular day.

During the observation, have your observation tool(s) and a pencil to take notes. Blend into the scenery of the classroom. Smile at the teacher and at the children when you enter, but do not elicit an official welcome or introduction. Do not interact with the children. If they come to you and ask you what you are doing, briefly say, "I am here to see what children learn." You need to remain unobtrusive so you can see the interactions in the most authentic way.

Plan to spend a couple of hours in the classroom. It is important to observe formal teaching activities as well as informal teaching activities. Examples of formal activity might be a math lesson to a small group, a read-aloud to a large group, or individual teaching of writing. Informal activity might be waiting in line to go to the bathroom, mealtime, or transitioning from circle time to going to the gym. In a good early childhood classroom, all these times should be "teaching times."

Leave the classroom only if there is an emergency that cannot wait. Do not use your cell phone. You need to send the message that you take this observation seriously. This builds your credibility when you give feedback.

Family and Coworker Surveys and Teacher Self-Evaluations

Distribute surveys to coworkers and families in individual envelopes. Ask for them to be returned within a week. Designate a special box or shelf for returning the surveys. Do not expect a 100 percent return. If you get half of them back, you will have enough information.

Distribute the self-evaluation tool for teachers at the same time you distribute the other surveys. Teachers do not need to give you their self-evaluations in advance of your performance review meeting. Taking the self-evaluation will help them prepare for the evaluation meeting with you. Ask them to bring their self-evaluations to the meeting.

Children's Outcomes

Review children's outcomes gathered by the program. Ask the teacher to bring assessment documents as well as work samples from the children to the evaluation meeting.

Step 4: Analyze the Results

With this process you will have information from five sources: yourself, teachers, families, coworkers, and children's learning outcomes. Your task is now to review all the data so you can examine the quality of the three aspects of a teacher's job: acts of teaching (what the teacher does), results of teaching (what the children learn), and professional behaviors (behaviors that make a teacher a good worker). To review and analyze the data:

- Organize the data from the various sources by creating a folder for each teacher.

- Tabulate the family and coworker surveys and summarize the responses.

- Score any assessments and observation tools you have used.

- Look for patterns.

Analysis is a very valuable part of the process. Don't rush it. Use this time to list the teacher's strengths and weaknesses according to the data. Look for similarities, as well as differences, in the data from the various sources. Come up with nonjudgmental, probing questions to ask the teacher that might help you both figure out solutions to weaknesses during the meeting. You will finish analyzing the data with the teacher at the evaluation meeting.

Step 5: Communicate the Results

Ms. O. teaches second grade. She has good rapport with the children. Her classroom is productive and calm. Parents love her. She follows the curriculum. Her students have good scores in reading and math. She has perfect attendance, almost never a sick day. She gets along with her colleagues.

Ms. B., a kindergarten teacher, has good rapport with the children. Parents love her. She does not follow the curriculum. The children who came in the fall with good scores are continuing to show progress and are getting better. The children who came in with low scores are staying low. They are not making progress. Ms. B. gets along with her colleagues.

Ms. A. teaches preschool. She does not have good rapport with the children. Her classroom is chaotic. Parents are concerned about her lack of communication. She does not follow the curriculum. Most of the children are not on target to be ready for kindergarten. She has perfect attendance, almost never a sick day. She has frequent conflicts with her teaching assistant.

Ms. T. is a toddler teacher. She has good rapport with the children. She provides fun activities for the children. Parents are concerned about the number of incident reports they receive. The classroom has the necessary safety features, but parents wonder if Ms. T. supervises and redirects the toddlers appropriately. She has good attendance.

Four teachers, four situations. These examples reflect the possible range of evaluation results you may need to communicate to individual teachers. More than likely, the performance review for Ms. O. will be the least challenging, and the review for Ms. A. the most challenging, but all four teachers need honest and sensitive feedback in order to maintain or improve their teaching quality.

Before the Meeting

Set an appointment for the meeting with the teacher well in advance so you both have time to prepare. Pick a time convenient for both of you. Plan to schedule one to two hours for the meeting.

Prepare for the meeting by reviewing your data analysis and organizing all of the sources of data in the teacher's evaluation folder. Refresh your memory about areas that are satisfactory as well as areas for improvement. Come with a positive and nonjudgmental attitude, ready to problem solve and collaborate with the teacher.

Ask the teacher to prepare for the meeting by reviewing her self-assessment, reviewing the results of children's assessments, preparing examples of student work, and bringing any other data or ideas she feels would be useful during the meeting. Encourage teachers to be involved in this process and to communicate their own expectations for their work. A performance review is an appropriate time to clarify discrepancies in expectations.

During the Meeting

Hold the meeting in a private space to minimize the chance of interruptions. If possible, have the meeting at a table that allows you and the teacher to sit at a ninety-degree angle from each other. That way, you can face each other—though not directly—and can look at data together. A table also gives you the ability to take notes.

Focus the meeting on analyzing and discussing the data rather than on passing judgment on the teacher as a person. As discussed in chapter 2, data is a relationship builder. It unites two people—who join heads and eyes—to look together at the same information. Focus the meeting on whatever data you and the teacher have collected for this performance review, which may include children's assessment results, classroom observation results, examples of student work, photographs, videos, teacher's notes, and so on.

The meeting should not be a one-way monologue from the education leader to the teacher but rather a professional conversation about what is going well in the classroom and what needs improvement. Make sure to listen and ask questions. Use questions to help teachers clarify, explain, and reflect—not to interrogate them. Here are behaviors to avoid during the meeting:

- **Rushing:** "I just have a few minutes . . ."

- **Jumping to a concern:** "There is something I need to tell you . . ."

- **"Why" questions:** "Why did you . . .?"

- **Judgment:** "I notice it wasn't very helpful when you . . ."

- **Sarcasm:** "Where did you get such a bright idea?"

- **Comparing to other teachers:** "Ms. P. does it this way . . ."

- **Comparing to yourself:** "When I was a teacher, I . . ."

- **Using absolutes:** "You always . . . ," or "You never . . ."

These are behaviors that work well:

- **Begin the meeting by thanking the teacher for participating.** She is taking the time out of her day to be a part of this process.

- **Acknowledge good work first.** Starting with the positives will help set the tone for the meeting.

- **Ask the teacher what is going well in her job.** Give her time to talk and explain her perspective.

- **Ask the teacher what is not going well in her job.** Or ask her what she would like to change. This is an effective approach to address concerns. More often than not, the concerns of teachers mirror those of leaders. Therefore, it is the perfect opportunity for sharing, collaboration, and problem solving.

- **Focus on the benefits and consequences for children.** This reminds both of you that the goal of teaching is that children learn. Reinforce a cause and effect perspective.

- **Ask for clarification.** At appropriate times say, "Tell me more . . ." or ask, "How did that go? What might be helpful in this situation?"

- **Listen attentively, nod, and smile.** This shows empathy and interest.

- **Use action-oriented words.** Words might include *growth*, *achievement*, *development*, *progress*, *success*, *accomplishment*, *challenge*, *manageable*, *future*, *plan*, *expectations*, *teamwork*, *results*, and *support*. These words help one visualize positive solutions.

- **Remain calm.** Maintain your composure even if you find yourself getting anxious or angry. This is a time to assess a situation that may need more problem solving.

Always end your meeting with a plan that includes clear goals for improvement that you can follow up on in future observations. These goals should be SMART:

- **S**pecific,

- **M**easurable,

- **A**chievable,

- **R**elevant, and

- **T**ime-bound.

The end of the meeting is also a time to offer resources and professional development opportunities that might be a good fit for the teacher's needs.

Document the plan for improvement, the teacher's current accomplishments, and other important information from the performance review. Both you and the teacher should have copies of this summary at the end of the meeting. An example performance review summary follows (see page 75). A reproducible version of this form can be found in the appendix.

Performance Review Summary and Plan

Name: _____   Date: _____

We have reviewed three areas of performance: acts of teaching, results of teaching, and other professional behaviors.

Accomplishments (notes for each area of teaching, using the checklist):

Areas of growth (what the teacher needs to do to grow professionally):

Plan as the result of this meeting (SMART goals—may relate to one or more areas of performance):

1.
2.
3.

Teacher responsibility and timeline:

Supervisor responsibility and timeline:

Follow-up meeting on:

SARA, *Center Director*

Sara used the Performance Review Summary and Plan with Ms. T, the toddler teacher. Sara filled out the first two sections (Accomplishments and Areas of Growth). During the meeting, both Sara and Ms. T discussed and agreed on the plan and the repository and timeline sections. ▪

Performance Review Summary and Plan

Name: Ms. T.   **Date:** March 15

We have reviewed three areas of performance: acts of teaching, results of teaching, and other professional behaviors.

Accomplishments (notes for each area of teaching, using the checklist):

· Positive feedback from colleagues.

· Some positive feedback from parents on Ms. T.'s friendliness. Also concerns—see below.

· Children's outcomes using Teaching Strategies GOLD show several children have high motor skills.

Areas of growth (what the teacher needs to do to grow professionally):

· Parents have concerns about safety. Four parents mentioned they had received incident reports about their children tripping over toys or running into furniture. No serious injuries were reported, but they felt some of the bumps and bruises could have been avoided.

· Room arrangement is not adequate.

· Teacher needs to adapt curriculum to children's high energy.

· Identified blind spot in classroom with large cabinet.

Plan as the result of this meeting (SMART goals—may relate to one or more areas of performance):

1. Continue positive rapport with children and colleagues.

2. Address safety immediately.

3. Revise curriculum to address children's high energy and interest in exploring.

Teacher responsibility and timeline:

· Tomorrow: change location of shelf to eliminate blind spot so children can be seen at all times.

· By next week: review lesson plan to include safer activities that are developmentally appropriate for toddlers. Use resource book Infant and Toddler Experiences by Hast and Hollyfield. Focus on "Chapter 4: Playing with Curiosity" and "Chapter 7: Fostering Coordination."

· Every week: choose and implement two new activities. Repeat successful activities that the children like.

Supervisor responsibility and timeline:

· In two days: visit the classroom to see new furniture arrangement.

· Monitor incident reports. Discuss each with teacher.

· Continue to observe classroom every two weeks for fifteen minutes.

· Send a letter to parents informing of positive changes in classroom.

Follow-up meeting on: May 15 to follow up on how goals are met.

Step 6: Conduct Follow-Up Reviews

Post-meeting reviews are crucial to maintaining and building trust in the evaluation process. It is not just teachers who need to follow through by working toward the goals you establish together. Leaders must also do their part. Follow-up might include a cycle of observations and coaching done by the supervisor or a person assigned to be a coach for a particular skill. For example, if a teacher's students have low scores in math, and the observation showed that the teacher did not teach enough math lessons, or did not do them well, this teacher might receive math coaching for the next four months.

A schedule for follow-up observations is set during the evaluation meeting. It is important to maintain it. If resources are offered (books, articles, materials, or a registration to a workshop), they should be given immediately. Make sure to give teachers autonomy to implement the goals within the timeline. The leader's job is to be positive that actions will happen, while continuing to be alert.

After the follow-up observation (and any subsequent follow-up observations), you will need to schedule another meeting with the teacher to review the teacher's progress toward the goals. You may only need thirty to forty-five minutes for these reviews. From there, you can revise the goals if the teacher has met or exceeded expectations, or if the teacher has not met the goals, work with the teacher to come up with new solutions for achieving the goal.

◆ ◆ ◆

The purpose of performance evaluation is to help teachers reflect on their jobs so they continue to improve their practice. It is not just a managerial responsibility; it is a leadership responsibility. You lead the teachers to become accountable for the results of their work. If you consider the parallel process, you are an important role model. You are like the teacher in the classroom who scaffolds children's learning and coaches them to success.

ADDRESSING PERFORMANCE PROBLEMS

JON, *Principal*

Jon found himself in a tight situation. The teacher in Preschool B left abruptly when she had to go on bed rest for a difficult pregnancy. Jon had hoped for several more weeks to find a substitute during the maternity leave, but now it was urgent. Two candidates were available on short notice. Their qualifications were good. One interview did not go well. The other was not stellar, but it was fine. Under pressure, Jon decided to hire teacher Bob.

From the beginning there were some red flags. Bob was late twice. Each time he had an excuse. Each instance caused scrambling to cover the classroom for ratio. It made the teaching assistant angry. In the classroom, Bob seemed to develop good rapport with the children. This was a relief to Jon. However, he did not follow the schedule and curriculum Jon had handed him. The day was a free-for-all. Behavior problems started to emerge. In just three weeks since he'd hired Bob, Jon was getting concerned and second guessing his decision. ■

Whenever a supervisor has a concern about an employee's ongoing performance, he needs to follow his intuition. He needs to use his wise mind and follow appropriate and ethical practices—and not just hope things will get better on their own. Here are some guidelines to help you think about what, when, and how to address performance issues.

When to Address a Problem

Act when you first notice a problem. Taking action right away can be difficult as most supervisors have a good heart and hope things will get better on their own. Unfortunately, it rarely happens that way. Avoiding problems can also be the result of having too much to do or not having the skills to know what to do. Occasionally, leaders are afraid of making the situation worse by intervening, so they work with the positives and ignore the negatives. To help you decide when immediate intervention is needed, assess the problem against the following four criteria; if any of these are true, action is warranted:

1. The behavior of the teacher affects the learning of children.

2. The behavior of the teacher affects his or her performance, the performance of coworkers, or the performance of your center or school.

3. The conditions of employment are not followed.

4. Legal requirements are violated.

JON, *Principal*

Jon analyzed the situation with teacher Bob:

- Item 1: Bob had good rapport with the children, but the children's learning was being harmed by Bob's disregard for the curriculum and the lack of schedule.

- Item 2: Bob's tardiness had a negative effect on the teaching assistant and on the smooth running of the center.

- Item 3: Arriving on time is explicitly stated in the employee handbook, so this condition was not met.

- Item 4: Bob's tardiness affected the legal requirement for adult–child ratio.

Jon knew the situation required an intervention. ■

How to Address a Problem

Effective communication is essential, especially when there are problems to solve. When addressing performance problems with a teacher, it's best to invite the teacher to a formal meeting. Do not try to grab the teacher on the fly. This conversation needs to happen in private and should not be rushed.

Allowing silences and pauses throughout the conversation is a powerful way to give the teacher time to think. Throughout the conversation, use a calm tone of voice. Expressing anger—even if you feel angry—may generate defensiveness and prevent a productive conversation from the start. At the same time, being overly friendly can confuse your message as well. Here are some other tips for addressing problems with teachers and examples of how Jon might use them in his meeting with teacher Bob:

- **Take notes.** In the example, Jon might let Bob know from the start that he plans to take notes because he wants to remember what Bob says. Even as he takes notes, Jon should continue to maintain regular eye contact with Bob.

- **State your concerns overtly.** Jon might say, "Bob, I want to talk about two concerns I have regarding attendance and the curriculum."

- **Describe the problem and its effects.** Regarding the attendance problem, Jon might say to Bob, "I noticed that you have been late two times already. This affects the children and your colleagues. It lowers the quality of the center. When you were late, we had to delay breakfast time."

- **Remind the teacher of the program expectations.** Jon might remind Bob of the expectations about attendance and about using the curriculum.

- **Use objective tools.** Jon might mention standards from the employee handbook, the *NAEYC Code of Ethical Conduct*, the *Early Childhood Generalists Standards*, or the state's early learning standards to support the program's expectations.

- **Ask open-ended questions.** Questions might include, How does it happen? Can you say more? What would be helpful to you? What plan should we make?

- **Do not interrupt.** This time should be a dialogue between the teacher and the leader, with each side taking turns speaking and listening. To reduce the chance of interrupting, Jon might decide to focus on taking careful notes while he is listening to Bob.

- **Acknowledge the other person's feelings.** Jon might make statements to Bob such as, "I see how it can be difficult" and "I imagine that must be challenging."

- **Stick to the subject.** If the conversation starts to stray from the subject, Jon could say something such as, "Bob, it is important that we stay on this topic. We have to solve this problem."

- **Be patient.** The teacher needs time to sort through his feelings and to understand the cause and effect relationships of his actions.

- **Create a win-win resolution.** Offer resources and a willingness to solve the problem together. End the meeting with a plan of action that works for both of you. In the example, Jon might write down steps he and Bob have come up with to solve the problem:

  - Bob will set his alarm clock for earlier in the morning to ensure he has enough time to prepare and arrive to the center on time.

  - Jon will highlight the parts of the curriculum Bob should follow.

  - Bob will continue to follow the daily schedule of the last teacher to offer stability for the children.

  - Bob and Jon will meet every Thursday for thirty minutes to review the lesson plan for the next week. Bob will explain his plan and will ask for resources and ideas then.

- **Be clear about consequences.** Fairness, objectivity, and clarity are all necessary to providing appropriate support. Your role in addressing performance problems is to help the teacher succeed. In order to succeed, teachers must understand the consequences of not following through on their end of the resolution. You have to be clear about what will happen if there is no improvement. Document the consequences in writing, and include actions and a timeline at the bottom of the document. Jon documents the following:

- Bob and Jon will implement this plan immediately starting on November 1.

- The plan will be reviewed formally in three months, on February 1, based on the weekly meeting schedule.

- This plan is nonnegotiable. If not followed, it will result in loss of employment.

Addressing performance problems may be uncomfortable, especially at first, but doing so is essential if you want to maintain quality in your setting, both quality in teaching and quality in children's education.

What to Do When Performance Problems Do Not Improve

Ethical performance evaluation requires informing the teacher of the problem, setting expectations, and providing guidance and resources. If an employee is not able to improve, it should not be because the supervisor gave up or ignored bad performance. That is neglectful leadership. The education leader has to be rigorous and compassionate, yet steadily work toward progress. The purpose of addressing performance problems is not to punish, but to help teachers improve and learn practices and behaviors that are better.

If the employee does not improve, then it may be necessary to dismiss this person according to the code of ethical conduct (P-3.11). In the end, the education leader is responsible for children's education, and an ineffective teacher harms children's growth as well as their futures.

EVALUATION AS RESPONSIBILITY

In a recent public debate, members of a teachers' union proposed the elimination of academic testing. They argued that assessing children's learning was taking too much time, and that this time would be better spent on instruction. In this district, the results of teaching (the academic testing) showed that a great number of children were failing.

Children are not the cause of their own academic failure. Academic failure is the result of teaching that does not fit children's ways of learning. Sometimes children cannot learn because teachers do not know what to do. They do not know what strategies the children need. Sometimes children do not learn because teachers choose to follow their own personal choices or interests rather than best teaching practices. The children in this district were failing but *not* because teachers were spending too much time assessing children's learning and not enough time teaching. The children were failing because the teaching they did receive wasn't high quality.

To improve academic outcomes, these children didn't need *more* teaching, they needed *better* teaching. But because this school district didn't regularly assess teaching quality and couldn't analyze the patterns, they didn't make the connection between learning outcomes and teaching quality. The union's proposal to eliminate academic assessments was a misinterpretation of the limited data they had.

This is why teacher evaluations are a serious responsibility. Evaluations are a part of "excellence in all areas of practice" (Copple and Bredekamp 2009). And they reinforce the idea that professional progress is a step toward a program's goals for children. We have to engage in the teaching evaluation process with the same spirit that we engage in evaluations of children's learning. Doing so is necessary to ensure an excellent education for children.

Reflection Questions

1. After reading this chapter, how do you envision doing teacher evaluation in your program? What ideas will you use to complement what you already do?

2. How do you make the parallel between assessing children and evaluating teachers? Have a discussion about this topic with your staff.

5 TOOLS *and* TECHNIQUES *for* SUPPORTING TEACHERS

Teachers know that evaluating children's learning is not enough. Evaluations simply tell teachers where children are in their learning and measure improvement over time; evaluations do not nurture improvement on their own. Instead, teachers use the data from evaluations to inform the next step of providing appropriate instruction to support children's learning. Likewise, evaluating teachers is not enough to foster improvement. Education leaders must use the data from evaluations to come up with the best ways to support teachers' professional growth. Two ideals of the *NAEYC Code of Ethical Conduct: Supplement for Early Childhood Program Administrators* (NAEYC 2011a, 5) describe these responsibilities well; according to these ideals, education leaders are responsible for doing the following:

1. "To coach and mentor staff, helping them realize their potential within the field of early childhood education" (I-3.3).

2. "To encourage and support continual development of staff in becoming more skilled and knowledgeable practitioners" (I-3.5).

Supporting teachers' growth includes training, coaching, and mentoring through relationship-based practices that pay attention to teachers as people and as professionals. Coaching, mentoring, leading, and supervising have elements that overlap (Glickman 2002). A good education leader is more effective when she is also a good coach. A good coach has to be directive and supportive at the same time.

Being an education leader gives you some power to make things happen toward your mission of improving the quality of teachers' practices. But you cannot simply make demands of teachers in your effort to support them. This would not be a relationship-based practice. A domineering leader who delivers strict and inflexible rules does not help workers feel their best and do their best. Workers may feel scared into following the rules but may not understand the reason for them. In this environment, teachers do not feel professional—and they will act accordingly. This situation does not usually get good results.

The opposite approach is a permissive style, where there are no rules, few expectations, and total freedom. Permissive leaders don't provide much, if any, direction. This environment often leads to anarchy. Nobody knows what's going on. This approach delivers poor quality too.

A better approach is to be authoritative. An authoritative leader follows and provides rules that are explicit. Within the boundaries of these rules, however, there is freedom to try new ideas and activities. The authoritative leader evaluates teachers on a regular basis so rules and methods can be adapted as needed.

As you work to implement the ideas for support in this chapter, monitor your style of leadership and assess if you lean toward being domineering, permissive, or authoritative. Consider whether your style is helping or hindering your efforts to support teachers and improve the quality of teaching in your program.

SUPPORTING PROFESSIONAL DEVELOPMENT AND PROFESSIONAL ENGAGEMENT

Two important guiding principles for evaluating and supporting teachers are to

1. enhance professional competence and

2. facilitate involvement in the field of early childhood education.

Supporting professional development and engagement are essential components of meeting these principles. Use the data from your evaluations to pinpoint areas where teachers might benefit from professional experiences outside the walls of your center or school. Simply signing up teachers for trainings or buying tickets for them to attend professional conferences is not enough to improve skills if there is no follow-up (Fuller 2011).

Pay Attention to Teachers' Training in Relation to Data

In-service training is mandated for topics such as health or child abuse prevention. By law, a minimum number of hours are usually required per year. For topics related to child development, curriculum, or instruction, renewal certification or continuing education units are given regardless of what the person actually needs to learn to improve or increase her skills. Individuals decide which workshops to attend and often sign up based on personal convenience, such as their schedule or interests.

The result is that teachers often get better at what they already do well. For example, if a teacher has no interest in early math but has a special interest in children's literature, she might choose to take classes on literature to learn about more books and authors. This may increase her ability to find interesting storybooks, but it does not increase her skills in teaching early math. This situation is common and remains undetected unless education leaders diligently monitor assessments of children's learning and carefully evaluate teachers' practices so they realize children are not learning particular subjects.

Pay attention to the trainings teachers attend in relation to data from evaluations so you can guide teachers to the professional development experiences that will most improve their skills. As the leader who has looked at the children's outcomes and who has observed the classrooms, you know what is going well and what needs to improve. Together with your teachers, you can design a model of professional development that includes individual needs and whole staff needs.

After the trainings, facilitate the connection between what teachers learned and the impact on children's learning. Teachers must be made responsible for the information, or the trainings will have been for naught. You might do so in these ways:

- Organize a "PD Show-and-Tell" where teachers present short summaries of what they have learned, relating it to the needs of their children.

- Set up a private blog or Facebook page where teachers can post examples of children's learning, based on suggestions from the training.

- Notice the new strategies that teachers use, and give them affirmations.

Educate Yourself on Best Practices

During training workshops, I often hear teachers say, "I wish my director was here to hear this." Leaders in early childhood education should have a strong knowledge of current best practices and standards—and not just the big words on paper, but the fine details of what best practices look like in action. Directors and principals who support teachers have responsibilities to run their programs as a business, but they are also education leaders responsible for supporting teachers' growth. It is surprising how few directors or principals attend the workshops their teachers attend, which means that when teachers come back with new knowledge, they cannot get enough support from their leaders because their leaders don't have the information to do so.

While attending every training with teachers is impractical, attending some of them is not. And you can work to continually educate yourself on current research in other ways too:

- Attend conference workshops that are most relevant to the needs of your program.

- Set aside formal time to read the journals and books that pile up on your desk.

- Connect with your local professional association to join a leaders' study group.

You must be knowledgeable about current best practices so you can be credible. Being knowledgeable also prevents a disconnect from developing between your joint goals with teachers and your actions in supporting those goals.

Show Interest in What Teachers Learn in Training

If you are not able to go with your staff to a training, I recommend organizing a debriefing at the next staff meeting. Then you can be formally updated about what teachers learned, rather than informally through comments about how much they enjoyed the workshop. Offer your support to implement the new information by having teachers complete a simple survey about the training in which they can write down the most important points they learned as well as what might be needed to apply their new knowledge with the children. Follow up consistently with teachers after you collect this information. Doing so will show your interest and commitment to their professional development. On page 87 is an example of what a post-training survey might look like. A reproducible version of this form can be found in the appendix.

Post-Training Survey

Name: _____   **Date:** _____

Topic:

Two things (knowledge and skills) I learned that I want to use in my classroom:

1.

2.

Three things I need to make that happen:

1.

2.

3.

Timeline. I would like to review these ideas and make a plan:

☐ NEXT WEEK   ☐ IN ONE MONTH   ☐ IN THREE MONTHS

Facilitate Teachers' Involvement in Professional Associations

Many teachers do not know about organizations such as the National Association for the Education of Young Children (NAEYC), the National Child Care Association (NCCA), or the National Head Start Association (NHSA). Further, they do not know that there are local and state chapters. They are not familiar with the resources that these associations have and do not meet colleagues outside of their center or school. This lack of connection to the greater early childhood field contributes to professional isolation.

Many education leaders do not see their role in facilitating teacher engagement in professional associations, which means they are missing opportunities to support teachers in becoming more grounded in their field. By encouraging engagement, you can help teachers meet others who are dealing with the same joys and challenges and help them feel part of a larger movement. Here are some suggestions to facilitate the connection:

- Share information about professional associations available in your area.

- Have a library of child development and curriculum books to check out.

- Have a library of old and current magazines and journals from professional associations.

- Share magazine and journal articles that are relevant to their daily work.

- Organize reading clubs of these articles, where teachers discuss the ideas.

- Provide time and full or partial registration fees to attend conferences.

- Contribute to full or partial association fees for teachers.

NURTURING A REFLECTIVE PRACTICE

The day-to-day pace of working with young children is reactive. One has to make decisions all day long. The average teacher makes thousands of decisions a day. Many decisions are related to physical safety; these decisions are stressful, especially when involving infants and toddlers. An important job of education leaders is to provide opportunities for teachers to take pause and reflect on these many decisions—to reflect on their practice in order to assess and improve their own work. Doing so is a part of the guiding principles to enhance professional competence and to provide appropriate direction and resources.

Reflective practice takes time and often remains just a good intention. But there are ways you can be efficient when nurturing this skill, for example, by adding regular times for reflective practices to teachers' daily and weekly routines. This practice could take place at the beginning, middle, or end of the day or week.

For regular group reflective practice, you might post two sheets of chart paper on a wall of the staff lounge with two prompts, such as these:

ONE THING I AM THINKING ABOUT	ONE THING THAT WENT WELL TODAY IN OUR CLASSROOM

Encourage teachers to write their thoughts in either category and check it daily. You will be able to use these ideas at your next staff meeting for further group reflection.

For regular reflective practice with individuals, use simple paper forms or e-mails to pose a weekly question or prompt, and encourage sharing by e-mail or paper by the end of the week:

- I am proud of . . .

- I have learned . . .

- I am still wondering about . . .

Asking powerful questions is another way (and one of the best ways) to help teachers think deeply about their work. Powerful questions guide teachers to reflective solutions during the numerous and diverse interactions you have with them throughout the year, such as when they come to you with a challenge or when you are analyzing data together. Questions should never be about blame or asking, "Why did you . . .?" These should be nonjudgmental questions to help teachers think deeply so they can improve their skills. The power of these questions is in how they pull out cause and effect relationships. They often address the thinking and feeling aspects of reflection. Here are some examples of kinds of questions you can use to help teachers reflect:

- **Anticipation questions:** What might happen if . . .? What if it doesn't work out the way you wish?

- **Assessment questions:** What do you think is best in this situation? How do you feel about it?

- **Clarification questions:** Can you say more about . . .? What does it feel like?

- **Exploration questions:** What may be your options for approaching . . .? What is just one more possibility?

- **Fun perspective questions:** What was humorous about this situation? What could make it fun?

- **Implementation questions:** What is the action plan for this situation? What do you need to get the job done?

- **Cause and effect questions:** What happened when . . .? What would happen if . . .?

- **Learning questions:** What did you learn from this situation? If you had to do it over, what would you do?

- **Outcome questions:** What do you want? What will it look like?

- **Resources questions:** What resources would help you decide? What is available now?

- **Planning questions:** What will be needed to get this task done? Now what?

- **Big-picture questions:** In the bigger picture, how important is it? So what?

COACHING

Coaching is a relatively new strategy in the field of early education. It is an effective way to provide support for all teachers, but it's especially effective for teachers who need extra support. These teachers may be at the beginning of their careers, or they may have several years of experience but are learning a new way of teaching. Sometimes coaching happens as a part of the formal evaluation process, but more often, coaching happens outside of the supervisory process to help teachers achieve specific goals of more limited scope. Coaching will help you practice all five guiding principles of evaluation and support.

A coach is assigned to a teacher or a team of teachers. The coach uses a relationship-based process to support and scaffold a teacher's professional performance based on data from observations and evaluations. The process includes "various combinations of questioning, listening, observation, reflection, feedback, prompting, modeling, and practice" (Lutton 2012, 85). The length and intensity of coaching may differ. It may happen weekly for a few weeks or monthly for a school year. Basically, coaching is an intentional method of support that includes a specific protocol of actions and responses by a trained coach.

Resources for Coaching

I recommend three coaching resources for you to explore.

1. **Practice-Based Coaching** is the model adopted by Head Start, created by the National Center on Quality Teaching and Learning. The website offers several practical checklists and tools to implement coaching: https://eclkc.ohs.acf.hhs.gov/hslc/tta-system/teaching/development/coaching.html.

2. *The Early Childhood Coaching Handbook* written by Dathan D. Ruch and M'Lisa L. Shelden is a hands-on guide that makes coaching easy to understand. The book is published by Brookes Publishing, www.brookespublishing.org.

3. *SEEDS of Coaching* is a coaching model that most intentionally uses the parallel process approach of treating teachers as teachers are expected to treat children. The acronym *SEEDS* stands for a coach who is **s**ensitive to teacher's needs, **e**ncourages teachers to grow, **e**ducates teachers by providing resources, and helps teachers **d**evelop by practicing. The result is the last S, teachers whose **s**elf-esteem is strong. Created by Kate Horst, it was first tested at the University of Minnesota when Kate and I were co-coordinators of the Minnesota Early Literacy Project. It has since been used successfully in the pre-K Reading Corps Project and other projects nationwide. More information can be found at: www.cehd.umn.edu/ceed/projects/earlyliteracyproject/default.html.

Rules for Coaching

Coaching is most effective when certain rules are followed. Keep these in mind as you prepare to coach your teachers:

- **Climate:** Warm and positive relationships happen when coaches and teachers engage in social conversation. They show enthusiasm for the work they are doing together with upbeat comments. They have a sense of humor that is respectful.

- **Sensitivity:** Sensitive coaches are aware of the teachers' levels of skill. They listen actively and respond appropriately to teachers' concerns and ideas.

- **Teacher perspective:** Coaches take the teachers' perspectives during challenging moments. They say they understand, and they do. They empathize with teachers' challenges while at the same time helping them problem solve. They give teachers time to practice, and they check in to see how it is going along the way.

- **Leadership:** Coaches state the expectations clearly. They are consistent in setting goals and in expecting results. They redirect teachers' thinking or behavior when they stray from these goals.

- **Efficiency:** Coaches are organized and efficient. They have a coaching plan, and they make the most of the limited time available for coaching.

- **Format:** Coaches use tools for observations and discussions. Teachers are familiar with these tools. They understand the objectives.

- **Analysis:** Coaches focus on understanding concepts that are important in early childhood education. They facilitate analysis. Teachers learn about cause and effect.

- **Feedback:** Coaches focus on the process of learning. They scaffold learning by providing specific information about correct and incorrect practices. They encourage teachers to persist.

Notice that these practices echo and reinforce the actions to take to create a caring community of workers (described in detail in chapter 2): developing professional relationships with teachers, setting common goals, communicating effectively, encouraging collaboration, and modeling caring and empathy.

In a federally funded professional development project I co-led at the University of Minnesota in 2001–2003, we found that teachers who received coaching were, indeed, better able to sustain literacy-rich classrooms than teachers who did not. Consequently, the children learned more and better. I have worked in several coaching projects over the years and have conducted surveys to find out how teachers felt about the experience. Teachers who get fair and constructive evaluation followed by supportive coaching are consistently satisfied. This is what they say:

- "At first I was scared to be videotaped and to be evaluated. But it is such a good way to 'see' my work!"

- "I am more confident in my teaching than before. I wasn't sure what I was doing right."

- "I have learned new information about early literacy, child development, and classroom management."

- "I appreciate knowing where our program is going. Before this I had no idea."

- "I like learning new skills and strengthening the skills I already have."

- "I have a stronger sense of accomplishment when I review and I see that I have met my goals."

- "I have learned to look at problems by asking questions with my coach."

- "I enjoy the camaraderie of working with my coach and my classroom team."

- "I feel I can share ideas and the responsibility for children's learning with my coach. I am not alone!"

The teachers' comments give us a glimpse of what coaching can do for them. If we coach effectively, teachers feel respected, learn new skills, have goals and a sense of direction, gain self-confidence, and share responsibility. Ultimately, they talk about being part of a community of workers.

Use Data for Coaching

The coaching process should always center on data: collecting it, analyzing it, and reflecting on it. Coaches typically look at data about children's learning, observe teachers in action, give feedback to the teachers, and ask them to reflect on their practices. As coaches and teachers work together, they continue to set goals to reach the desired results. It is a continuous improvement process. Coaching may be focused on content, such as literacy or math, or on classroom management or curriculum preparation.

The Coaching Protocol: Four Steps

JON, *Principal*

In teacher Rose's classroom, the children's vocabulary scores are very low in the winter benchmarks, and Jon wonders why the children aren't progressing. To evaluate the problem further, he uses a classroom observation tool that measures the quantity and quality of language modeling and practice; if little evidence of language modeling and concept development is apparent, the scores will be low in these areas. In addition, he asks the teacher about her own observations. In the end, Jon will have enough information to begin coaching teacher Rose. The coaching will not be based on his ideas alone, but on well-rounded data. ▪

The coaching protocol has four main steps: pre-observation, observation, planning the post-observation conference, and the post-observation conference. This process is similar to that of formal evaluations, but it is not about overall performance; instead, coaching focuses on a specific issue or skill that the teacher is working on. As illustrated in the example above, the focus might be on language development and increasing language use in the classroom.

- **Step 1: Pre-observation.** Plan the classroom observation with the teacher. Remind her of the instrument you will use for the observation and whether you plan to videotape her.

- **Step 2: Observation.** Arrive on time. Blend into the classroom. Take notes that describe the evidence you will need to discuss with the teacher.

- **Step 3: Planning the post-observation conference.** Review your notes and prepare briefly before the post-observation conference. Conduct the review within a couple of days of the observation.

- **Step 4: Post-observation conference.** Describe your observations using evidence from the tools used. Give affirmations on the items that were positive. Engage the teacher with open-ended questions. Help the teacher think about the relationship between teaching and learning as you look at children's data. Finish the conference by setting goals. In the last five minutes of the conference, write a plan of action with the goals and set a time for the next observation.

At the end of step 4, you and the teacher should establish clear goals and a plan for moving forward. The most common formula for setting goals is the SMART model described earlier. This is how Sara set SMART goals with a teacher and teaching assistant she was coaching.

SARA, *Center Director*

Sara: Thanks so much for your time. When I came last Tuesday, it was very nice to see the children in your classrooom engaged in interesting activities. But when we looked at the data, we saw the children's vocabulary scores were low. We felt they needed more opportunities for language learning and decided I would observe the use of language in your room, using the ELLCO section 3 on the Language Environment. I did, and now I want to give you some feedback. My notes show the children do not talk much. One of the teachers talks often with the children, and one does not. Here are the examples I recorded [*shows the times and examples*].

Teacher (T) and Teaching Assistant (TA): We have a lot to do in the classroom, like clean up.

Sara: [*short silence; listening*] Is it possible to clean and talk with children at the same time?

T: I guess so . . .

Sara: How could it happen?

T: We could get a couple of kids that are around and let them know what is happening?

Sara: Kind of like a running commentary?

TA: Yes, like that . . .

Sara: Would you do that all the time?

T: No, only when we set up for snack.

Sara: Okay, that is a good start. Could you also do it at the end of snack?

T and TA: Okay.

Sara: I'd like to make that a goal and then come back next Wednesday and observe again. Let's write this goal down: We will talk to the children who are nearby when we are setting up and cleaning up snack [**R**elevant]. We will talk about what we are doing and about what the children have been doing [**S**pecific]. We will use running commentary during snack setup every day [**M**easurable]. When will you start?

T: Tomorrow. [**T**ime-bound]

Sara: Thanks so much. I look forward to coming back next week and seeing how running commentary happens during snack. [**A**chievable]

The coaching protocol is cyclical in nature: after coming up with a plan and setting goals for improvement in step 4, you return to step 1 to plan your observation of how well the improvement plan is working.

Create a Coaching Plan

Coaching effectively means having a plan. On page 96 you will find a planning form that may help you structure your coaching sessions. You may use it as is or adapt it to your own style. A reproducible version of this form can be found in the appendix.

Coaching Plan

Activity to be observed:

Tools used during the observation (such as children's data, videos, observation notes, and scores):

Last goal set:

Actual description of the observation and score, if appropriate:

Analysis of observation:

What happened? What does it mean for children's learning?

What needs to continue?

What needs to change?

New goal reflecting the analysis:

What is the desired result?

What will occur?

When will it occur?

Date for next observation:

Date for next post-observation meeting:

FACILITATING MENTORING RELATIONSHIPS BETWEEN TEACHERS

Another effective approach to supporting teachers is mentoring. Mentoring is "a relationship-based process between colleagues in similar professional roles, with a more-experienced individual with adult knowledge and skills, the mentor, providing guidance and example to the less-experienced protégé or mentee. Mentoring is intended to increase an individual's personal or professional capacity, resulting in greater professional effectiveness" (Lutton 2012, 84).

Mentoring is less structured than coaching. It can be very informal; anyone can find a person that they admire and ask to be their protégé. However, in order to support teachers well, I recommend creating a system that establishes a more formal relationship between experienced and new teachers. Mentoring is a valuable way to encourage collegiality. Being a mentor is also a nice professional challenge for experienced teachers who are ready to share their expertise with less experienced colleagues. Overall, it is a good way to foster improvement throughout a school or program.

MONIQUE, *Education Coordinator and Coach*

Monique has set up a basic mentoring system that is effective for her program. She works in several sites and her time is limited; she knows that a more elaborate system would have been difficult to organize, and she wanted to get going quickly and efficiently. After discussing it with teachers and assistant teachers, she set up a mentoring program that works for all. Monique is the coach for the teachers, and the teachers are the mentors for the assistant teachers. Each team is given thirty minutes every other week for mentoring time.

In order to start this mentoring program, a staff meeting was dedicated to a training workshop on mentoring. Three ground rules were established: (1) sign an agreement, (2) document goal setting and follow-up, and (3) address concerns directly with Monique, if disagreements develop.

The list of questions (see page 90) was discussed as a tool to use for working with each other. They decided to pilot this plan for three months and evaluate it. A simple mentoring agreement was developed to act as a reminder of what to do. A reproducible version of this form can be found in the appendix. ■

cont'd

Mentoring Agreement

Mentor: SR

Mentee: AP

Date: March 3, 2014

Arrangements for meeting or contact

When: every other Tuesday between 7:00 and 7:30 AM

Where: in the classroom

How: latte day • will bring our own

Ground rules for working together

1. We will start and end on time.
2. We will review previous notes and write new notes each time.
3. We will limit to two goals.

Main goals we are working on (no more than three)

1. Set up classroom the night before so it is ready in the morning.
2. Planning to read new book on art activities and get ideas.

Accomplishments

- Getting room ready the day before has worked for 2 weeks now, yeah! Will continue.
- Have not looked at book yet—will begin next week.

Initialed:

SR _____   AP _____

MENTOR   **MENTEE**

There is a continuum of approaches for mentoring (and coaching too) that you may want to discuss with your mentors. A directive approach is on one side of the continuum and a nondirective approach is on the other. The directive approach includes these same techniques but with more emphasis on making suggestions or giving advice. In the nondirective approach, the dominant techniques include listening, reflecting back, and summarizing. The best approach depends on the personality and philosophy of the mentor (or coach), as well as the needs of the teacher and the urgency of the situation. I recommend that your mentors not be rigid in their approach. It is best to be flexible.

COUNSELING

According to principle P-3.10 of the *NAEYC Code of Ethical Conduct: Supplement for Early Childhood Administrators* (NAYEC 2011a, 5), leaders should "provide guidance, additional professional development, and coaching for staff whose practices are not appropriate. In instances in which a staff member cannot satisfy reasonable expectations for practice, we shall counsel the staff member to pursue a more appropriate position." Sometimes a teacher does not want to or cannot improve her performance. In this case, she will need more intensive support. The relationship-based process applies in counseling too, but with an even more focused approach. Like other forms of support, the goal of counseling is to improve the teacher's skills. However, based on the teacher's needs, the support process may result in changing the direction of her professional life. Teaching is not for everyone.

SARA, *Center Director*

When Sara arrived at the center, she found a teacher who could not garner the energy and the discipline for teaching children every day. She was very interested in children's learning, but she was not interested in preparing activities or doing all the other necessary tasks of running a classroom. It was frustrating for her colleagues, who accused her of being lazy. It was demoralizing for her too. This situation had been going on for two years. Sara set up a performance review in the fall. They made a coaching plan. No improvement happened during winter quarter. They set up bi-weekly meetings to continue to discuss options and possibilities. By the middle of spring the teacher had decided that teaching was not her calling. She left the center and enrolled in a graduate program to become a researcher in child psychology. She could not be a teacher but found a way to keep her interest in children satisfied. This is a success story. ■

EMPOWERING TEACHERS TO SUPPORT ALL LEARNERS

Teachers' sense of efficacy is the belief that they make a difference. Teachers with a high sense of efficacy are confident in their ability to impact children's learning. Children have better behaviors and better academic achievement when their teachers have a good sense of efficacy (Protheroe 2008). These teachers exude confidence in their skills. Their spoken and unspoken message is, "It is hard to learn, I know. But I also know I can teach you, and together we'll find a way." The children interpret this as "I am teachable; I am respected as a learner." This is a nice combination of messages. It is strong and powerful.

This sense of efficacy comes not just from individuals' innate personalities but from other important sources, such as the levels of guidance and feedback they get early (Fives and Buehl 2010). Most importantly, it's not *positive* feedback that increases efficacy, but *constructive* feedback that helps them solve problems and examine what they are doing and how they could do it differently. In this way—with constructive feedback—you can help teachers develop the sense of empowerment to teach all children.

SARA, *Center Director*

Sara had a perplexing data review meeting with the teachers in preschool B. In the assessment system they use, the charts are colored: red for far from target, yellow for near target, and green for on target. The classroom chart was mostly red. Yet, when Sara asked the team how the children were doing, they responded, "very well" and pointed to the children who were in the green. When she asked what made them think that, they said that these children were doing well because they had good families who are engaged and read to them at home. What about the other children then? They did not have an answer, except the feeling that the children in the red columns just could not learn. And they did not see how these children could be helped. They did not feel that they could help as teachers. Their sense of efficacy was low.

Sara thought of her kit of powerful questions: If these children cannot learn, what are their options? What might happen if we just stopped teaching these children? What do you want for these children? What would you need to help you find a way to teach them?

She did not expect instant answers for these big questions. She also used silence so the meaning could sink in. As a matter of fact, they ran out of time, and the meeting ended in silence. But they picked up the conversation the following week. The teachers acknowledged they wanted the children to learn, but they did not know how to differentiate instruction. Sara then gave them some strategies to try. ■

Teachers' beliefs about children can affect their efficacy, which can affect how, what, and who they teach. Cultural or socioeconomic differences, for example, are often confused with developmental or behavioral problems. We cannot let that happen, because it contributes to a low sense of efficacy; teachers may think, "I cannot teach these children, because they are just too different from me." Part of the support we need to give teachers is to help them overcome their prejudices and their misconceptions. We need to develop teachers who are culturally responsive so they feel confident and empowered to teach *all* children.

JON, *Principal*

When Jon arrives in classroom B for an observation, the teacher greets him with stories of the children: J. is having a difficult time because his mom just changed jobs and works nights. M's dad was arrested last week. O. has a new baby brother and he is jealous. It is important to pay attention to the whole child and be aware of what is going on in the lives of our young students, but these stories appear to be excuses for why J., M., and O. are not learning or have challenging behaviors. Jon wonders what this teacher believes about the children. Does she believe these children can be taught? What assumptions is she making about these children's behaviors and their ability to learn? What is her own sense of efficacy? Does she believe she can teach the children in her classroom?

Jon's most effective strategy is to not follow the teacher's line of thinking. He does not validate the negative comments. Instead, he is patient and sticks to the problem: The children are not learning. He uses questions and silence to help the teacher reflect: What do you want to see happen for the children? What do you need to get the job done? What options do you have to improve the problem? ■

Sometimes what looks like low efficacy is actually a teacher having misguided or faulty information about children's abilities. They believe that some children are not capable of learning, so they give up (Ritchie and Gutmann 2014).

Helping teachers identify and question their beliefs and assumptions about children when needed and improving teachers' sense of efficacy can be challenging, but doing so can help teachers achieve a new level of skill, confidence, and empowerment.

KEEPING MORALE POSITIVE

I want to end the chapter by highlighting techniques for keeping up morale. Sometimes morale is described as the best fuel for good work. Internal or intrinsic motivation comes from the person's inside and helps maintain morale. But external rewards and recognition are also important for refueling workers' well-being, especially in professions that are demanding and offer low pay.

Many strategies are effective in promoting positive morale. These strategies provide support quickly and consistently and are essential for day-to-day interactions. You can find ways to boost morale in writing and verbally, one on one or as a group. The choice of medium and environment depends on your temperament, the temperaments of your teachers, the size of your team, and the resources you have. Try adding some of the following strategies into your daily work with teachers:

- **Tell teachers what they do well.** Rather than general praise, "Good job at story time today!" they should hear specific affirmations: "You are a very expressive reader. This keeps the children very engaged during story time. They learn more that way."

- **Say thank you.** These two simple words are not used often enough, and yet they are so important! Thank-yous need to be about something specific and said with meaning, for example, "Thank you for talking to Paul's mom this morning and reassuring her about his toilet training progress" or "Thank you for sharing the article about separation anxiety. I am grateful to have knowledgeable colleagues like you."

- **Explain the "why."** One's work life in education can be a blur of mandates, rules, and expectations. It is easy for teachers to forget priorities and purpose. The "why" for decisions or policies must be explained. It is a respectful way to keep teachers engaged and motivated. Here are some examples of explaining the "why":

  - *Why do we need to keep the toddler classroom uncluttered?* "Putting the toys back on the shelf periodically has two reasons. One is educational: it helps toddlers find the toys and organize their play better. The other is safety: adults and children won't trip over them on the floor."

  - *Why do we need to have lesson plans?* "Lesson plans are not just paperwork. They are a tool to help teachers focus on what children need to learn and to prepare appropriate activities. Having a lesson plan is not enough if it is not implemented. When it is, it shows that the teacher is truly intentional."

  - *Why do we need to pay attention to the early childhood standards?* "The early childhood standards are based on early education research, and they give us guidance on what children must learn. It is an important map that everyone in our center must consider."

- **Be a team leader.** Teams are built with daily effort, fair rules, respect, and commitment to common projects or ideals. In challenging situations, teams become strong when there is open communication and joint problem solving. I invite you to think about the traits of a good team leader as you work with your team: a good team leader is optimistic, sincere, solution-oriented, fair, kindhearted, and courageous. Find these characteristics in yourself, and use them with confidence.

- **Promote a gossip-free environment.** Gossip is a common challenge in early childhood programs (Mooney 2012), and it undermines morale. As the leader, you need to make your site a "gossip-free zone" and be explicit about it. My best argument is that adults are models for young children. When there is tension, children pick up on it. That is unacceptable, as it affects negatively the social-emotional development we proclaim is so important. Remain alert to it, however, so you can address discontent directly and quickly.

- **Bring playfulness to work.** Team leaders celebrate success too. They share genuine fun times with their teachers. I recently was at a meeting of early educators who shared ideas to create playfulness at work. Some of the suggestions they had were doing the happy dance; wearing costumes according to the season or the holiday; instituting special days such as crazy hairstyle day, hat day, or funny shoes day; distributing playdough during staff meetings to use to relieve stress during discussions; and sharing funny or sweet cartoons about teaching young children. You may have other examples. These activities work well when the spirit is positive and individuals do not feel pressured into participating.

Reflection Questions _____

1. Think of a coach or a mentor you have had in your life. What did that person do to help you learn a skill or get better at it? How can you apply these characteristics in your work with teachers?

2. Review the support techniques described in this chapter. Which would be helpful to you at this time? How would you modify the technique to make it relevant to your situation?

6 DIFFERENTIATING SUPPORT

Developmentally appropriate practice (DAP) means teaching in ways that

1. "meet children where they are, as individuals and as a group" and

2. "support each child in attaining challenging and achievable goals" (Copple, Bredekamp, and Gonzalez-Mena 2011, 3).

For teachers, this relates to paying attention to the needs of the large group of children *and* to each individual child. It means having a vision and goals for what all children need to learn and finding specific ways to teach and motivate each child—differentiating instruction—based on her needs (such as where she is in her learning and her preferred learning style). No two children are alike.

Likewise, not all teachers are the same, so it makes sense to apply the same concept of differentiation to your work of supporting teachers; meet teachers where they are and support them in attaining challenging and achievable goals. Doing so will help you meet the guiding principles of providing appropriate direction and resources and enhancing professional expertise. As you read this chapter, think about your own community of workers and how you might best support them as a group and as individuals.

THE EARLY CHILDHOOD EDUCATION WORKFORCE

Approximately 2.2 million workers earn a living caring for and educating children younger than age five (Child Care Aware of America 2013). About half of these workers are employed in centers or family child care homes. The other half are paid relatives, friends, and neighbors. About 97 percent are women. The US Bureau of Labor Statistics (2014a) estimates the ten-year job outlook for child care workers is at 14 percent. This is higher than average growth for our field, and the demand for child care is expected to increase until 2020.

Early childhood is increasingly understood as preK–3 in the field of elementary education, meaning preschool through third-grade classrooms that are part of the K–12 system (Kauerz 2006, 2010; NAESP 2005). PreK–3 alignment is a new and evolving trend in the field and is not yet established in all states. From kindergarten to third grade, all the teachers are college educated, with master's degrees in some cases. In other sectors of the early education field, such as child care centers and Head Start, the education of workers is more varied. About a third of center lead teachers are college graduates, 47 percent have some college, and 20 percent have a high school education or less. In the classroom assistants group, 12 percent have a college degree, 45 percent some college, and 43 percent high school or less (US Bureau of Labor Statistics 2014a). This is an amazing array of formal education among the early childhood educators who serve millions of children from birth to early elementary school.

The compensation for this workforce is varied too. The average salary of an elementary school teacher is $41,520 per year, compared to $24,410 for a preschool teacher in a child care center (US Bureau of Labor Statistics 2014b). Infant and toddler teachers may make even less money. Assistant teachers may make even less—they are often scheduled based on the number of children on site and may work irregular hours. Most child care employers do not provide benefits such as health care or vacation time. These marginal working conditions are in seeming contradiction to the predicted growth of the field and the increasing public discourse on the importance of child care and early education. These conditions may be some of the reasons the turnover rate for child care workers is between 25 and 40 percent (Center for the Child Care Workforce 2002).

In addition to having diverse working conditions and varied levels of formal education, early childhood educators have a wide range of skills and professional experience. They include people of varying ages and temperaments and come from different personal and cultural perspectives. Yet, from the perspective of children, all adults in the classroom are teachers! From the perspective of the research and the standards, it seems that way too. We have to be sensitive to the support we provide to our diverse population of early childhood teachers so they can best support children's learning. Our support cannot be one-size-fits-all. We each have to tailor our methods of support to our own unique group of teachers as well as to the individuals within the group. What follows are some ideas for how you might approach differentiating support based on the background of your staff.

SKILL LEVEL

As in any occupation, early childhood teachers come with varying levels of skill and talent. Alongside this variance, we know that the teacher is the most important factor in children's learning. A skilled and effective teacher will help children learn at a faster and better pace, regardless of children's backgrounds. Less effective teachers will actually set children behind (Tucker and Stronge 2005).

With good support, teachers with average skills can become effective enough to take children from the fifty-ninth percentile to the seventy-eighth percentile in a two-year period (Sanders and Rivers 1996). This is wonderful news for us in the business of supporting teachers! We can meet teachers where they are in their skill level and find specific ways to foster improvement based on their strengths and weaknesses.

Stages of Skill Development:
Novice, Advanced Beginner, Competent, Expert

Just as teachers scaffold children's learning to provide the appropriate level of support and challenge based on where they are in their learning, you can scaffold the support you give to teachers so you offer the right level of challenge based on their current skill level. Even though skill development is not linear, predictable stages happen that can guide your approach:

- **Novice:** A novice teacher is new to the field and has limited skills. If asked what she needs, she might say, "Just tell me what to do. Give me a curriculum and recipes for success." This teacher wants to follow a curriculum plan, as she is not able to plan one herself. She needs limited choices so she does not become overwhelmed.

- **Advanced beginner:** This teacher might say, "I can take this curriculum and choose some activities." This teacher can modify some of the activities but not on the spot. If the children become antsy during reading time, she chooses to stop reading and have everyone jump up and down. This teacher is better able to identify what to do to improve. However, she may have too many ideas, so she needs a leader who can help her choose the most effective strategies.

- **Competent:** This teacher might say, "I can plan and know what children need to learn individually." This teacher picks up the pace to make the reading more interesting. If children become antsy during reading time, she still follows her lesson plan, making adaptations for individual children. This teacher needs a leader who encourages her and gives her additional resources to keep her motivated.

- ◆ **Expert:** This teacher can plan both for the large group, individual children, and small groups. This teacher might say, "I just read this great article about the project approach. Let's have a planning session and figure out how to do it." She initiates planning and engages other staff. She needs a leader who helps her channel her interests and energy as a peer mentor. If her expertise is far above that of her colleagues, she may need some guidance so she does not overwhelm them.

To keep teachers motivated and happy in their work, it is crucial to provide the right amount of support and challenge based on their skill level. Too little support and too much challenge will make teachers feel less confident. They may just give up trying and revert to what they know. That happens when leaders buy expensive curriculum packages that are difficult to implement, and provide intensive three-day training workshops without follow-up. After the initial excitement, nothing much happens. The curriculum gets forgotten.

At the same time, too much support and too little challenge also decreases teachers' motivation to improve. Teachers feel disrespected. They wonder why they have to attend so many workshops on a topic they feel they know. They might confuse knowledge with practice, and they might complain that they "know this stuff," but it may not show in their daily practice. These are signals to leaders that they are providing the wrong kind of support. Instead of more knowledge, the teachers may need coaching to practice what they know. Or if they already practice what they know, they may be ready to take on the challenge of becoming a mentor to a less experienced peer.

Teachers' Skill Awareness

There is another way of looking at skill development that is well worth using in our field. In our efforts to learn any skill, we progress from being unconsciously unskilled to consciously skilled. As an unconsciously unskilled person who watches a figure skater on TV—with her graceful glides and pirouettes—I can easily tell myself that this skill looks doable. All I have to do is buy good skates, practice a little, and I will look just as good on the ice. With my first fall on the ice, however, I become consciously unskilled. I am now aware that this skating business is much more difficult than I thought. I am hurt physically from falling, as well as mentally from the realization that I just don't know how to skate.

Depending on my personality, I may persevere on my own and get better. Or I may give up altogether because I have no one to help me learn. Or I will be lucky and find a friendly and skilled person to give me good tips so I can learn the skills. The first time I can do several minutes of gliding by myself, I begin to feel consciously skilled. I am aware of my starting skills and become hopeful that I will get better. With more practice and continuing encouragement, I will become unconsciously skilled. I will lace my skates, get on the ice, and go with confidence. Every time I want to learn a new move, I will get back to my consciously unskilled then skilled states again. Overall, I will have learned that I can learn.

SARA, *Center Director*

When Sara hired her, Kim was a young teacher who had just graduated from a university with a degree in child development. Kim was twenty-three years old and already had extensive experience working with young children as a babysitter, camp counselor, oldest of ten cousins, and teaching assistant while in school. She had taken good courses in child psychology, early literacy, and curriculum development. She was enthusiastic and said she loved children, especially toddlers; they were her favorite age group.

At this point, Kim was unconsciously unskilled. She did not know that she did not know how to manage a classroom of twelve toddlers and a teaching assistant. After two weeks in this classroom, however, Kim found herself overwhelmed and crying in Sara's office. Three biting incidents in one week had made her realize she was unskilled in working with toddlers. Yes, they were cute, but they seemed unpredictable and dangerous now, little monsters to be tamed.

Knowing of the progression of skill awareness, Sara did not let teacher Kim blame the children or herself. She acknowledged the challenge. Teacher Kim did not have the skills to teach toddlers to be safe, but these skills could be learned, and Sara would help her. She encouraged Kim and redirected the energy toward learning how to prevent, minimize, and eliminate biting. They developed a plan. At the end of the next week, there had been only one incident. Sara met with Kim the following Friday and talked about the success. Kim felt consciously skilled. She was using the techniques they had discussed and they were working. By the next week, there were no more incidents. Kim had learned an important teaching skill, and she was feeling confident. ■

Knowing where teachers are on the continuum of being unconsciously unskilled to consciously skilled in any area can help you respond to teachers' challenges with understanding and the appropriate level of encouragement and support, as Sara did in the example above. The best way to find out about teachers' skill awareness is to listen and ask questions. What is the teacher saying about herself and about the children? If she seems unrealistically optimistic, she is likely to be unconsciously unskilled. If she looks defeated, she may be entering the consciously unskilled stage, which is very uncomfortable. It will be a temporary phase, however, if the education leader pays attention and provides support so the teacher is not permanently discouraged. The education leader's job is to help the teacher move to being consciously skilled. The first step is to acknowledge that dealing with a new job, a new situation, or a new skill is challenging and also normal. Giving reassurance and specific tips for action will scaffold the teacher to the next level of confidence, to being consciously skilled.

Barriers to Skill Development

Two common situations in early childhood affect the skill development progression and confidence: one is high turnover and the other is too many initiatives. With high turnover, teams are constantly formed and reformed. At any one time, the new person may be at a different stage than the other people on the team. For example, a novice teacher may join a team of competent teachers who have little patience to show him what to do. That might result in this person not learning from his peers. The education leader needs to see the barrier and provide individual support as well as make an explicit plan with the entire team.

The second situation occurs when a teacher may be functioning at a high level, but her program decides to implement new initiatives without providing adequate support. I recently conducted a workshop for Head Start education coordinators who wanted to learn techniques for supporting their teachers. We did an exercise tallying the number of new initiatives in their programs in the past three years. The initiative could be new curricula, new regulations, new techniques for brushing teeth, new assessments, and so on. When they counted all the new items, the average was ten per program. Some were brought upon by the national Office of Head Start, some by their state agency, and others by their own program leaders.

Too many changes at once will affect entire staff, not just individual teachers. Major changes bring whole teams from a highly functioning, competent state to the beginning of the skill development cycle again. They may feel bad about themselves—not knowing how to use the new curriculum or apply the new regulations—and lose their motivation as a group. If this happens too often, they just "wait it out" until the next initiative comes along. Leaders must invest time and explicit support to help teachers become consciously skilled again with any new initiative.

> **MONIQUE,** *Education Coordinator and Coach*
>
> Monique understands this situation well. In the last two years, her Head Start program has had three new initiatives created by the federal office, two initiatives from her state office on quality, and three initiatives begun as a result of local grants that her program received. All in all, in three years, eight initiatives have taken place. Some are related but with different twists. For example, there is a new math curriculum, a new literacy curriculum, one family literacy program, and one language and movement research project. They are all about language and literacy, but each with a different spin. The teachers have received many hours of training, but they still cannot integrate it all in their heads. ■

For each initiative, trainers come to the program with only their perspective. They do not integrate their ideas into the other initiatives already in progress. This puts teachers in the difficult position to figure out integration on their own. It is an unfair burden on teachers. It really is the responsibility of administrators and education leaders to explain and map out how the initiatives work together, identifying which ones should be eliminated to accommodate others. Introducing new initiatives is not necessarily a bad thing, but initiatives should be implemented selectively and gradually—and with explicit plans for support. Monitoring and responding to these kinds of barriers to skill development is a big part of an education leader's job. Consider your entire team of teachers, and take actions to minimize the consequences of high turnover and too many initiatives.

FORMAL EDUCATION

All teachers in public school–readiness programs have bachelor's degrees. Head Start and Early Head Start programs have the expectation that at least one-third of their teachers have a bachelor's degree. In the general early childhood workforce, an associate degree from a community college, the national CDA certification, and a high school education are more common. Some research shows that children learn more when their teachers have a higher level of education (Barnett 2011). In practical terms, these teachers have higher literacy and language skills, which are a definite advantage.

However, the research is not conclusive (Bowman 2011). While formal education may be an indicator of quality, and a good goal to have, it is not *always* a factor in quality. And all teachers, no matter their level of formal education, need support from their leaders. For example, one of your teachers may have wonderful intuition relating to children but little formal education on child development and early literacy. You might choose to send this teacher to child development and literacy trainings with her peers, and propose to observe her reading to children. Or you might lead a study group of new teachers on the topic of early literacy.

Another teacher may have taken all the required courses on early literacy, but may not have the classroom-management skills to keep a lively group of four-year-olds productive enough to learn what they need to. For this teacher, you might choose to videotape the classroom in action so you and the teacher can look at the data (children's behaviors) together and come up with solutions.

Education leaders can meet teachers where they are in their formal education and help them fill in the gaps where needed:

- Do not make assumptions about the relationship between education and skill level. Instead, look at the data regarding teaching quality.

- Provide more information on a topic to individuals, the large group, or a small group when you know there may be gaps in knowledge. Consider including video examples on the topic, or other media, to present the information.

- Demonstrate a skill in the classroom and ask the teacher to observe you and note what you do. Then provide follow-up information on the skill from authoritative resources.

- Allow time and space for a learning community of teachers to gather together to explore a topic.

EXPERIENCE

Years of experience is a factor you should consider when planning your approach to support. Experience can be a bonus or a disadvantage. Competent and motivated teachers with many years of experience will be an asset to a center. They bring personal and professional maturity to do their job and to mentor novice colleagues. Evaluating these teachers will be an upbeat process. However, if teachers with longevity have low skills, they can be challenging. They may be resistant to new ideas. In this case, they will need a thorough evaluation and sensitive support to make positive changes.

New teachers with low skills may be easy to support if they are enthusiastic about their jobs. They are likely to be open to your ideas and leadership. Either way, your role is to guide these new teachers' learning to fit the goals of your program.

Education leaders should consider teachers' years of experience when planning how best to approach support:

- Do not make assumptions about the relationship between experience and skills.

- Observe teachers, and consider the data before deciding on a course of action.

- Always ask teachers to reflect on their interests and professional goals at the same time that you provide direction about the program goals.

AGE/GENERATION

The age or generation of teachers in your group also needs to be considered. Much is being said about the different habits and expectations of baby boomers (born between 1946 and 1964), Gen-Xers (1965–1977), and millennials (1978+). At the same time, there are universal values about professionalism that apply to all. These universal values are a part of the quality in professional behaviors checklist in chapter 3.

Communication and use of technology may be the most obvious issue since millennials are more technology oriented. That's why you may want to expand your communication tools by adding texting to e-mail or paper memos for short messages. However, it is important to set the clear expectation that all employees are responsible to learn the information in the longer paper or electronic documents that you ask them to read.

JON, *Principal*

Jon is in his early forties. He supervises a teacher in her sixties, two years away from retirement. While she is open to new ideas for teaching and assessing children, she is slow to use technology. She resisted using the new web-based assessment data system to the point where it was a problem for the whole school. Her data could not be included with the other classrooms. This was a main topic of discussion in her evaluation.

The teacher offered to pay her young tech-savvy assistant to enter the data. This was an unusual solution to which Jon agreed reluctantly. The story ended well. When the teacher saw how easy it was to manipulate the data once it was entered, she became interested in learning more and learned to enter data herself. Now she is a convert. It took patience on Jon's part to get her there. He dealt with the issue during the evaluation and provided support afterward. ■

Without generalizing on the characteristics of different generations and the potential gaps in perception, it is still important to be vigilant. An eighteen-year-old assistant teacher is likely to react differently than a forty-year-old lead teacher. At the same time, both need to be held to the same ethical standards.

Here are some tips for supporting teachers of varying ages in your setting:

- Do not make assumptions about the relationship between age and skill level. Consider the data first.

- Make expectations clear for all.

- Communicate in various ways, electronically and in person.

- Provide visuals and Internet resources.

INDIVIDUAL DISPOSITIONS AND LEARNING STYLES

Are your teachers introverts or extroverts? An introvert is a person who is energized by having time alone to think. An extrovert is someone who is energized by verbally sharing ideas and discoveries. Both have good qualities. Introverts provide some calm, and extroverts provide some excitement.

Individual learning styles also affect how people behave. Visual learners prefer to read information, while auditory learners prefer verbal information. Your teachers' natural dispositions and learning styles affect how they react to and affect the climate of your center or school.

SARA, *Center Director*

Sara supervises a teacher who is very effective. They also get along well personally. Sara started to diligently put weekly written communication forms in the teacher's box, satisfied that she was given her affirmations. One day, in the course of a conversation, the teacher nervously mentioned that she was not sure how Sara felt about her work. She got the courage to say she was worried that Sara did not appreciate her work. That's when they discovered that, as an introvert, Sara preferred writing, but as an extrovert, the teacher preferred talking. Sara then made it a point to continue to write her notes, but also to say the same things verbally when she sees the teacher in person. ∎

Here are some tips for supporting your extroverted and introverted teachers:

- Provide information in multiple forms.

- Provide individual support in a manner best suited to the teacher's disposition.

- Make sure the staff room is always available for teachers who need a bit of calm space.

- Respect break times so all teachers have a moment to relax and re-energize in their chosen way.

CULTURAL DIFFERENCES

Early childhood education is an entry field to the workplace for immigrants and new workers, especially women. Even with low levels of education, it is easy to get jobs as classroom assistants or aides, so the workforce is culturally very diverse. It is important to reflect on how cultural backgrounds might impact communication and relationships. For example, consider the differing communication patterns of teachers from low-context versus high-context cultures. Low-context cultures, such as Northern European, Anglo-Saxon, or Asian, prefer a neutral conversation tone and controlled body language. Behaviors are measured, and people share professional ideas before they share personal feelings. In high-context cultures, such as Southern European, African, or Latino, people are more focused on facial expressions and body language. They tend to use personal information to illustrate professional ideas.

Cultural background refers not only to one's geographic and ethnic background, but also to one's experience in the individual family. Whatever the root of cultural differences, they may cause misunderstandings, as it is possible to misinterpret behaviors and comments. It takes effort and practice to build bridges of understanding (Shareef and Gonzalez-Mena 2008). The education leader can set the tone for comfort and openness.

MONIQUE, *Education Coordinator and Coach*
Although not her preferred style, Monique knows that the team from classroom B functions better when they start the weekly meetings with sharing personal stories before they move on to the order of business. Once they've talked about themselves, they are ready to talk about the details of their jobs. ■

Here are some tips for supporting teachers from varied cultural backgrounds:

- Make sure your employees reflect the diversity of children and families in your setting.

- Talk about cultural differences and similarities in daily conversations.

- Share ideas and beliefs from your own culture, and facilitate discussions of cultural differences and similarities.

- Listen to teachers' cultural perspectives related to their job of caring and educating children and working with families.

ASKING TEACHERS WHAT THEY NEED

You don't have to guess what teachers need. It is best that you ask teachers directly how they prefer to be treated and what they expect in their jobs. This can be done at the beginning of employment or anytime that is convenient. Here are some ideas to start.

Find Out What Teachers Need from the Beginning

Programs usually give new families intake forms when they enter the program to learn about the children to give them better support. I propose doing the same with new hires. On page 117 is a sample intake form for new teachers. A reproducible version of this form can be found in the appendix.

Assess Overall Job Satisfaction

Find out how teachers are feeling by distributing a job satisfaction survey. You can conduct the first survey at any time. Once you start, make it a yearly practice. In general, people are happy to be asked their thoughts, and they give candid answers that can be very useful. That means, of course, that the exercise needs to be treated with the utmost respect. You have to prepare yourself for taking the information and doing something about it. Even with a small staff, keep the survey anonymous. You have to maintain confidentiality and not try to guess who said what. It is not appropriate to talk to individuals to clarify what they have said. If you are unable to maintain this kind of neutrality, hire an outside consultant to conduct the survey.

An example of a job satisfaction survey is on page 118. A reproducible version of this form can be found in the appendix.

New Teacher Intake Form

Welcome to our center/school. We are very happy to have you on our staff. Please answer these few questions to help us get to know you better.

My strengths are:

I want to know more about:

I prefer communication by (check top two preferences):

☐ E-MAIL   ☐ TEXTING   ☐ WRITTEN NOTES   ☐ BULLETIN BOARD   ☐ IN PERSON

Two things very important to me in the workplace are:

When I am not at work, I enjoy:

Job Satisfaction Survey

Dear teachers,

I am checking in to see how our team is doing. From time to time it is important to slow down and reflect on our work together. Please respond to these ten statements by rating them with this scale. I will tabulate the answers and share the results at next week's meeting. Thank you for sharing your thoughts!

	ALWAYS	USUALLY	SOMETIMES	RARELY	NEVER
1. I am satisfied with my job.	☐	☐	☐	☐	☐
2. Staff meetings are useful.	☐	☐	☐	☐	☐
3. I feel respected.	☐	☐	☐	☐	☐
4. I am getting the help I need to do my job.	☐	☐	☐	☐	☐
5. My job is fun most days.	☐	☐	☐	☐	☐
6. I feel competent.	☐	☐	☐	☐	☐
7. We are a good team.	☐	☐	☐	☐	☐
8. I am clear on our goals for the children.	☐	☐	☐	☐	☐
9. Rumors and gossip are spread frequently.	☐	☐	☐	☐	☐
10. My daily work is manageable.	☐	☐	☐	☐	☐

I wish for more . . . (Please finish the sentence.)

I wish for less . . . (Please finish the sentence.)

A NEED FOR DIFFERENTIATED SUPPORT

In this chapter, I have presented a view of the early childhood workforce and the various factors you may need to consider when providing support. Given the diversity of workers, we need to think about differentiated support. Again, differentiated support means having a vision and goals for what everyone needs to know to do a good job and finding specific ways to motivate individuals. The vision and goals are spelled out by the professional standards and codes of ethical conduct. The way to support teachers to reach these standards is based on their individual needs: skill, experience, level of education, age, language, and culture.

Reflection Questions _____

1. Review the characteristics of teachers in this chapter and compare to the teachers with whom you work. What insights does it give you about your staff?

2. How many new initiatives have you had in your program? What has been the impact on your work and the work of your teachers? What insights do you have for the future?

7 MAKING *a* PLAN *for* EVALUATING *and* SUPPORTING TEACHERS

JON, MONIQUE, AND SARA, *Education Leaders*

Jon, Monique, and Sara all want to have a plan for evaluating and supporting their teachers, but they are at different levels of readiness.

December is nearing, and Jon has not had a chance to plan yet. He has barely had a minute to breathe, let alone start planning. Since September, he has not been able to hire a teacher's aide for one of the pre-K classrooms. Things are going well in kindergarten and first grade, but the second- and third-grade teachers have disagreements over the curriculum. He has promised himself to use the observation tool and self-assessment from chapter 1 right after winter break.

Monique is ready to start planning how evaluation and support will work in her program. Her biggest challenge is finding time. Due to a shortage of substitute teachers in her program, she is now the in-house substitute any time a regular teacher is absent. She has a meeting with her supervisor to problem solve her schedule. She will make the case that a thoughtful plan for supporting teachers will decrease absenteeism.

Sara has a plan. Applying for accreditation has increased her motivation. She is on a timeline to finish the accreditation paperwork and prepare for the site visit. ■

Yes, evaluating and supporting teachers is a good idea, but how can education leaders get started with limited resources of time, energy, and money? And once they find the resources, how can they supervise, coach, evaluate, and support in an efficient and effective way that respects teachers and enhances the quality of education for children? The answer lies in planning.

Think of your own situation. Is it similar to Sara's, Monique's, or Jon's? Given the responsibilities and challenges you already have, do you feel ready to plan? Know there is no perfect time to begin planning how to evaluate and support your teachers, but I encourage you to start now, even if it means starting small. Whether or not you have formal supervisory responsibilities, you will make a positive difference through your efforts.

To illustrate how to create a plan, we will follow Sara's story throughout this chapter. It should give you an example for planning you can use at your program. If your current situation feels more like Jon's or Monique's, fear not. You will find ideas for small steps you can take now, which you can build upon over time. As you read, think about the tools and techniques from earlier in the book that might work best for you and your program.

READY TO PLAN

Since the beginning of the book, we have used five guiding principles as the goals for effective evaluation and support of teachers:

1. create a caring community of workers,

2. enhance professional expertise,

3. provide appropriate direction and resources,

4. assess professional skills and growth, and

5. facilitate involvement in the field of early childhood education.

You've explored many ways to support these guiding principles, but these tools and strategies will only be effective if you are intentional in making them come to life. You need to find ways to *systematically* implement them in your organization every day.

Just as we expect teachers to have lesson plans to be intentional in teaching children, education leaders need plans to support and evaluate staff. The plan needs to be simple so it feels doable. To help you in this effort, I propose an easy guide:

1. Assess the situation in your setting.

2. Decide which principles are most urgent for you.

3. Write SMART goals.

4. Implement your plan.

5. Evaluate your plan.

Assess the Situation in Your Setting

Use the two assessments from chapter 1 (pages 12–13) as a place to start. These tools are fairly informal and not time consuming. Like most education leaders, you are probably extremely busy and harried. Your findings from these quick assessments will be enough to help you decide your initial priorities for evaluation and support. They will give you a quick picture of how well you are currently supporting and evaluating teachers and will show you which guiding principles need the most work.

SARA, *Center Director*

Sara reviews her self-assessment and observation of teachers from chapter 1. She creates a list to compare the results on both forms and separates out the items practiced always, usually, sometimes, and never. She formats the "never" items in bold.

GUIDING PRINCIPLES	SELF-ASSESSMENT		OBSERVATION OF TEACHERS	
	Always or Usually	Sometimes or **Never**	Always or Usually	Sometimes or **Never**
Create a caring community of workers	*I greet teachers every day with a positive comment.* *I provide comfort and assistance for personal and professional issues.* *I help resolve problems.* *I listen.*	*I smile, laugh, and am enthusiastic about our work with children, families, and colleagues.*	*Teachers greet one another every day.* *Teachers assist one another with personal and professional issues.*	*Teachers smile and make positive comments.* *Teachers listen to one another.*
Enhance professional competence	*I give feedback when teaching is not going well.* *I provide information and resources.* *I provide professional development to the group and individuals.*	***I give specific affirmations on performance.*** *I give feedback when teaching is going well.*	*Teachers know how to assess and analyze children's learning.*	*Teachers integrate previous experience with new knowledge received in professional development.* ***Teachers know the impact of their teaching.***

cont'd

GUIDING PRINCIPLES	SELF-ASSESSMENT		OBSERVATION OF TEACHERS	
	Always or Usually	Sometimes or **Never**	Always or Usually	Sometimes or **Never**
Provide appropriate direction and resources		***I communicate clear direction and objectives in multiple ways.*** *I am consistent with consequences.* *I use effective questions to encourage reflective practice.*		*Teachers make educational choices based on program objectives.* *Teachers know what quality is in our organization.* *Teachers understand and articulate the expectations and objectives of our organization.*
Assess skills and growth	*I assess classroom quality.* *I encourage teachers to persist even when the work is challenging.*	*I assess teacher skills.* *I scaffold teacher skills.*		*Teachers assess their own teaching.* *Teachers take risks, try new ideas, and evaluate them.*
Facilitate involvement in the field of early childhood education	*I help teachers feel connected to the ECE professional community.* *I share the teachers' interests and enthusiasm.*	*I actively engage teachers in making decisions for our center.*	*Teachers are connected to early childhood community.*	*Teachers mentor one another.* ***Teachers share their professional interests and enthusiasm with colleagues.***

Looking at these assessments, Sara begins to think about her current strengths and weaknesses in supporting and evaluating her teachers. ■

Decide Which Principles Are Most Urgent for You

The evaluation and support needs for every program will be different. After reviewing your results from the self-assessment and teacher observation tools from chapter 1, you should notice your program's areas of strengths and weaknesses. As you match this information to the priorities and agenda of your center, you will be able to pick the principles you want to work on first.

> **SARA,** *Center Director*
>
> Sara analyzes the results in her chart. She determines that there are no bold or "never" items for the principle of creating a caring community of workers. Even though her efforts in this area are not perfect, she has laid a good foundation for the caring people she leads in the workplace environment. The other principles all have some bold items, so they need more attention. Since she is pursuing NAEYC accreditation, she wants to focus on her weak areas of providing clear direction and resources, enhancing professional expertise, and assessing teachers' skills and growth. ■

Write SMART Goals

Once you have a broad sense of where you'd like to focus your attention, you need to come up with specific goals for your efforts. As mentioned in chapters 4 and 5, SMART (specific, measurable, achievable, relevant, and time-bound) goals have a better chance of being achieved than vague goals, so craft your goals accordingly. An example is provided on the next page.

SARA, *Center Director*

So far Sara has been looking at the broad picture. Now she applies detail to her goals. She chooses three items from the list and includes specific actions she will take, based on a timeline.

GUIDING PRINCIPLE	GOAL	ACTIONS	TIMELINE
Enhance professional competence	Give specific affirmations on performance.	Use the strategies in chapter 5 to give specific feedback to teachers in person and in writing.	Starting next week, February 1.
		Relate the affirmations to an authoritative resource, such as the early learning standards, to focus the affirmation on children's learning goals and quality teaching. For example, "After the reading of *Polar Bear, Polar Bear,* you showed the children the YouTube clips of the hippopotamus braying and the flamingo fluting. That was a very effective way to teach vocabulary. Thanks for being such a creative and resourceful teacher."	
		Use the weekly communication form from chapter 6 every other week.	
Provide appropriate direction and resources	Communicate clear direction and objectives in multiple ways.	Establish bimonthly Friday morning meetings; announce meeting schedule to teachers.	March 1
		Review accreditation process on my own to understand it.	March 15
		Announce process to teachers and reassure them that accreditation will not start until next January.	March 30
		Gather feedback from teachers about how they feel (survey).	
		Plan discussions every other week at meetings.	

cont'd

GUIDING PRINCIPLE	GOAL	ACTIONS	TIMELINE
Assess skills and growth	Assess teacher skills.	Focus the next professional development day on teacher evaluation.	April 15
		Plan an evaluation using information from chapters 3 and 4.	May 15–June 15
		Explain the concepts of acts of teaching, results of teaching, and professional behaviors (chapter 3) to teachers.	Conduct observations, 360 surveys (parent and coworkers).
		Describe the evaluation process and the tools we will use (chapter 4).	Conduct evaluation meetings June 20–30.
		Propose a timeline for teacher evaluations.	

Additional notes: Set up chart paper on easel in teacher's lounge with title "Fun at Work." Ask teachers to add their ideas of what would make work more fun for them.

Even though Sara feels that the principle of a caring community of workers seems fairly well met, it is an area of particular interest to her. So she decided to use the ideas in chapter 6 to ask teachers for ideas on activities they would like to do to have "fun at work." She puts a sheet of chart paper on the staff room wall for a week so teachers can write their ideas. She will follow up by having everyone rank their first choice. If some wishes are not possible, such as a retreat day in Hawaii, they will have a laugh together. ▪

Implement Your Plan

Once you have set your SMART goals, you have to get to it! Sometimes leaders feel like they have too many other important responsibilities, so the goals for supporting and evaluating teachers may have to wait. I would argue that making these goals a priority actually does make these other responsibilities go more smoothly. For example, a caring community will lessen conflict. And a good system for evaluation and professional development will result in more confident and competent teachers. The end result is likely to be less turnover, which makes the leader's job easier!

> **SARA,** *Center Director*
> Sara's motivation comes from the deadline for accreditation. The goal chart with the timeline makes it easy for her to move to implementation. She looks at the dates monthly and checks the items she has completed. Sara uses her sense of discipline to stay on task. She knows that teachers are the most important resources in her center. She sees the long-term benefits of improving her evaluation and support processes. ∎

Evaluate Your Plan

Evaluating your plan doesn't need to be complicated. The critical part is to remain intentional, just as we want teachers to be intentional in their efforts with children. To evaluate your plan, ask yourself four simple questions:

1. What actions were taken?

2. What actions were not taken? Why? (List the reasons.)

3. What went well?

4. What needs to change?

> **SARA,** *Center Director*
> This is how Sara answers the questions in June, when she has time to review her plan.
>
> 1. **What actions were taken?** I conducted the initial assessments and made choices about my focus. I set a timeline.
>
> 2. **What actions were not taken?** After an initial good start, I did not keep up with giving affirmations using learning standards. I still think this is a good idea. I will keep it as an objective for the next year.
>
> 3. **What went well?** I am most satisfied with the teacher evaluation process. It was a great way to get to know the teachers better. I have a new confidence in building the capacity of my team. Five of the six teachers had a positive response to the process.
>
> 4. **What needs to change?** One teacher was resistant to the evaluation process. She did not complete her self-evaluation and has a "just tell me what to do" attitude. I need to start counseling this teacher. I don't know yet if this teacher will stay on the staff. I also did not have time to achieve all my goals.
>
> This is Sara's first try at an evaluation and support plan. She is very satisfied. Her efforts fulfill the requirements for the accreditation. Some details did not happen, but she knows she is on the right path. ∎

TAKING SMALL STEPS

Jon's and Monique's stories at the beginning of the chapter are a bit different from Sara's. They may not have as much time or control to plan. They can, however, choose one aspect of the guiding principles to focus on, using the quality checklists from chapter 3 as a guide.

JON, *Principal*

Jon identifies that one principle needs the most attention: providing appropriate direction and resources. The new pre-K to third grade initiative is confusing everyone. He sets three goals: (1) learn more about the initiative himself so he understands it well; (2) hold biweekly staff meetings so all the teachers can be in the same room to share ideas and hear the same message; and (3) put the topic on the agenda so he and the teachers can discuss what the "pre-K–3 alignment" means for them as a school. ■

MONIQUE, *Education Coordinator and Coach*

Monique has a meeting with her administrators. They want her to focus on the principle of enhancing professional competence. They expect her to be the internal coach for her program, focusing on early literacy and math. They agree to hire a floating substitute teacher to free up Monique's time so she can provide the coaching. She will visit each classroom every other week and have a post-observation meeting with each teacher for forty-five minutes after the observation. ■

RECOGNIZING EVALUATION AND SUPPORT AS A GOOD TIME INVESTMENT

You might think a plan for evaluating and supporting teachers sounds very nice but worry about the time and effort you will have to invest. In my work, I always do time estimates for projects. It's a good way to gain perspective. To alleviate your concerns, I have calculated the hours it would take per year to adequately support and evaluate teachers.

Yearly Estimate of Hours to Evaluate and Support Ten Teachers in a Center or School

TYPE OF ACTION		TASKS	HOURS PER ACTIVITY	ESTIMATED TOTAL HOURS FOR 10 TEACHERS
Design and maintenance of plan for evaluating and supporting teachers			8 hours	8 hours
Group support	Staff meetings every other week	Preparation: 0.5 hour Meeting time: 0.5 hour	1 hour × 26 weeks	26 hours
Individual teacher evaluation	Evaluation	Observation: 2 hours Survey collection: 1 hour Data review: 1 hour Conference with teacher: 2 hours	6 hours × 10 teachers	60 hours
Individual teacher support	Follow-up reviews after evaluation	Follow-up observation: 0.5 hour Post-observation conference: 0.5 hour	1 hour × 4 times × 10 teachers	40 hours
Individual teacher support		Verbal or written affirmations: 5 minutes	5 minutes × 52 weeks × 10 teachers	43 hours
Subtotal				**177 hours**
Individual teacher extra support	Coaching or counseling	Additional observation: 0.5 hour Additional post-observation conference: 0.5 hour	1 hour × 6 times × 10 teachers	60 hours
Grand total				**237 hours**

Estimating the full-time work year of an education leader at 2,000 hours, we can calculate that 177 hours is about 9 percent of the education leader's time. The 237 hours (which includes the extra support for teachers who need it) amounts to less than 12 percent of an education leader's time. That leaves about 90 percent of a leader's time to devote to all the other responsibilities of the job. An education leader with more than ten teachers could delegate some of the tasks or provide less-intensive support.

An environment where teachers feel well evaluated and supported is an environment where there is less confusion, less conflict, more productivity, and more quality. It is a place where teachers are happier and more skilled. In turn, it is a center or a school where children learn what they came to learn. The time investment to create a system for evaluating and supporting teachers is very worthwhile. It will make the rest of your work easier.

Reflection Questions

1. Review your notes on self-assessment and observation of teachers related to the guiding principles from chapter 1. Which are in the "always/usually" column? Which ones are in the "sometimes/never" column? How do they inform the priorities for evaluation and support in your program?

2. What are the barriers to evaluating and supporting teachers? What are the opportunities? Make a list of each. How can you use the opportunities to overcome some of the barriers?

CONCLUSION

The quality goals for the field of early childhood education are clear: We want children to be safe and to learn every day, and we want teachers to be well skilled and well supported every day. We have to visualize quality in order to know how to get there. We have to see what it looks like. Then we can apply the strategies that work.

Quality is more than nice environments painted in bright colors and teachers in uniforms. It is more than nutritious snacks and diapering procedures. It is more than occasional professional development with no follow-up. Overwhelming teachers with new initiatives and grants with uncertain relevance to their daily work does not promote quality in early childhood education.

We know what quality is. The standards for teaching and learning already exist. We must use them consistently, make them come alive in our classrooms, rather than waiting for some magical solution. Quality resources should be dog-eared and worn from constant use. Instead I see these resources gathering dust on forgotten shelves in leaders' offices. The quality of teaching in our settings needs to be a primary focus, and we must work with teachers with care and empathy. I agree with early childhood education thought leaders like Stacie Goffin (2013) who assert that we all must organize in our thinking and actions so we have a coherent field of practice. We need the courage to be accountable for quality.

There is much hope. As education leaders, we are part of a brighter future. We must come together to agree that quality can improve, and then we can make it happen. At the center level, we must put in place a good system of hiring, ongoing evaluation, professional development, supervision, and coaching so our teachers perform at the best possible level. At the policy level, we need to work consistently to figure out better conditions for our teachers. Policy is the long-term goal. Center-level improvements are the immediate job. You can start today.

Early in my career, one of my bosses directed me to "get rid of" one of our teachers. When I asked what that meant he explained, "Just let her fall of her own weight." In his view, this teacher would surely fail and be easy to fire if we withdrew all forms of support. Once I recovered from the shock of such a blatantly unethical directive, I decided that the opposite was a better option. With proper evaluation, feedback, and support, the teacher could succeed. So I set out to prove this point. And it worked. She improved her skills and her behavior. She was able to retire with dignity after several more years in the program. When I analyze how this happened, I see that my plan included all the best practices I have been talking about in this book. Over the years, I have seen these strategies work consistently. I encourage you to try them too, and I wish you the very best success.

APPENDIX:
REPRODUCIBLE FORMS

These reproducible forms can also be found on the Redleaf Press website (www.redleafpress.org). To download the reproducible forms, simply navigate to the *Evaluating and Supporting Early Childhood Teachers* product page and click on the Web Components tab.

Observation: How Well Are Teachers Evaluated and Supported?

Read the statements below and then for about a week observe what teachers say and do during their daily interactions. Checkmark the appropriate box to indicate whether the statements are true for your teachers always, usually, sometimes, or never.

In my program, teachers . . .	ALWAYS	USUALLY	SOMETIMES	NEVER
Create a caring community of workers				
1. Greet one another every day.	☐	☐	☐	☐
2. Smile and make positive comments.	☐	☐	☐	☐
3. Assist one another with personal and professional issues.	☐	☐	☐	☐
4. Listen to one another.	☐	☐	☐	☐
Enhance professional competence				
5. Integrate previous experience with new knowledge received in professional development.	☐	☐	☐	☐
6. Know how to assess and analyze children's learning.	☐	☐	☐	☐
7. Know the impact of their teaching.	☐	☐	☐	☐
8. Are organized and intentional in their planning.	☐	☐	☐	☐
Receive appropriate direction				
9. Know what quality is in our organization.	☐	☐	☐	☐
10. Understand and articulate the expectations and objectives of our organization.	☐	☐	☐	☐
11. Make educational choices based on program objectives.	☐	☐	☐	☐
Assess skills and growth				
12. Assess their own teaching.	☐	☐	☐	☐
13. Take risks, try new ideas, and evaluate them.	☐	☐	☐	☐
14. Cooperate with and encourage one another, sharing spaces, materials, and ideas.	☐	☐	☐	☐
Facilitate involvement in the field of early childhood education				
15. Mentor one another.	☐	☐	☐	☐
16. Are connected to the early childhood education professional community.	☐	☐	☐	☐
17. Share their professional interests and enthusiasm with colleagues.	☐	☐	☐	☐

Self-Assessment: How Well Are You Evaluating and Supporting Teachers?

Read the statements below and then reflect on your own daily interactions. Checkmark the appropriate box to indicate whether the statements are true for you always, usually, sometimes, or never.

In my program, I . . .	ALWAYS	USUALLY	SOMETIMES	NEVER
Create a caring community of workers				
1. Greet teachers every day with a positive comment.	☐	☐	☐	☐
2. Smile, laugh, and am enthusiastic about our work with children, families, and colleagues.	☐	☐	☐	☐
3. Provide comfort and assistance for personal and professional issues.	☐	☐	☐	☐
4. Help resolve problems.	☐	☐	☐	☐
5. Listen.	☐	☐	☐	☐
Enhance professional competence				
6. Give specific affirmations on performance.	☐	☐	☐	☐
7. Give feedback when teaching is going well.	☐	☐	☐	☐
8. Give feedback when teaching is not going well.	☐	☐	☐	☐
9. Provide professional development to the group and to individuals.	☐	☐	☐	☐
Provide appropriate direction and resources				
10. Communicate clear direction and objectives in multiple ways.	☐	☐	☐	☐
11. Am consistent with consequences.	☐	☐	☐	☐
12. Use effective questions to encourage reflective practice.	☐	☐	☐	☐
13. Provide information and resources.	☐	☐	☐	☐
Assess skills and growth				
14. Assess classroom quality.	☐	☐	☐	☐
15. Assess teacher skills.	☐	☐	☐	☐
16. Scaffold teacher skills.	☐	☐	☐	☐
17. Encourage teachers to persist even when the work is challenging.	☐	☐	☐	☐
Facilitate involvement in the field of early childhood education				
18. Help teachers feel connected to the early childhood education professional community.	☐	☐	☐	☐
19. Engage teachers actively in making decisions for our center.	☐	☐	☐	☐
20. Share the teachers' interests and enthusiasm.	☐	☐	☐	☐

Weekly Communication Form

To: _____ **Date:** _____

From: _____ **Site:** _____

Recognition or something that was meaningful for me this week:

Concerns and recommendations:

Things I would like you to know:

I need your assistance in:

Checklist for Assessing Quality of Acts of Teaching

This checklist will help you get a general picture of the acts of teaching. It is a tool for observation and discussion. Review the seven acts of teaching and the evidence of quality for that act of teaching below. Observe your teachers and mark how often teachers show evidence of that quality.

The teacher . . .	ALWAYS	SOMETIMES	NEVER
1. Has an efficient and rich classroom environment			
• The materials are developmentally appropriate and organized for learning.	☐	☐	☐
• The classroom is uncluttered.	☐	☐	☐
• Children are able to access materials on their own.	☐	☐	☐
2. Manages the classroom effectively			
• The schedule for the classroom is developmentally appropriate with a balance of teacher-directed and child-directed activities.	☐	☐	☐
• Conflicts are rare and easily managed.	☐	☐	☐
3. Has a positive rapport with children			
• Children smile, laugh, talk, listen, ask questions, and help each other.	☐	☐	☐
4. Implements the curriculum as directed by the program or school			
• Schedule, activities, and materials reflect the curriculum in all learning centers (literacy, math, science, blocks, library, sensory, manipulatives, meals, circle, large and small groups).	☐	☐	☐
5. Prepares and writes lesson plans for all children			
• A written lesson plan is posted.	☐	☐	☐
• The activities reflect the lesson plan.	☐	☐	☐
6. Provides developmentally appropriate activities that are content rich			
• Children can do the activities at various levels of proficiency.	☐	☐	☐
• Children listen, talk, read, and write throughout the day.	☐	☐	☐
• Children learn by playing, exploring, and experimenting.	☐	☐	☐
7. Assesses children's learning			
• Assessments are developmentally appropriate.	☐	☐	☐
• Assessments are both observational and standardized tools.	☐	☐	☐
• Collected data reflects children's learning and behaviors (notes, photos, work samples, scores, videos).	☐	☐	☐

From *Evaluating and Supporting Early Childhood Teachers* by Angèle Sancho Passe, © 2015. Published by Redleaf Press, www.redleafpress.org.

Checklist for Assessing
Quality of Results of Teaching

This checklist will help you get a general picture of quality in results of teaching. It is a tool for observation and discussion. Review the five results of teaching and the evidence of quality for that result of teaching below. Observe your teachers and mark how often teachers show evidence of that quality.

The teacher . . .	ALWAYS	SOMETIMES	NEVER
1. Uses assessments to plan teaching			
• Collected data is organized in portfolios.	☐	☐	☐
• Data is analyzed.	☐	☐	☐
• Data is used to inform teaching at the group level and at the individual level.	☐	☐	☐
2. Recognizes children's growth and learning			
• Children's growth and learning is quantified.	☐	☐	☐
3. Supports children's learning intentionally			
• Children learn.	☐	☐	☐
• Progress happens.	☐	☐	☐
4. Shares with coworkers			
• Coworkers understand what the children are learning and how to support it.	☐	☐	☐
5. Shares with parents			
• Parents understand what their children are learning and how to support it.	☐	☐	☐

Checklist for Assessing Quality of Professional Behaviors

This checklist will help you get a general picture of quality professional behaviors. It is a tool for observation and discussion. Review the seven professional behaviors and the evidence of quality for those professional behaviors below. Observe your teachers and mark how often teachers show evidence of that quality.

The teacher . . .	ALWAYS	SOMETIMES	NEVER
1. Maintains safety practices			
• Does not use cell phone while on duty with children.	☐	☐	☐
• Follows all health and safety procedures (hand washing, diaper changing, toy cleaning, and so on).	☐	☐	☐
2. Has regular and reliable attendance			
• Absences are rare.	☐	☐	☐
• Absences are justified.	☐	☐	☐
3. Has positive relationships with parents			
• Parents are satisfied with teacher interactions.	☐	☐	☐
• Disagreements with parents are handled respectfully.	☐	☐	☐
• There are no ongoing conflicts with parents.	☐	☐	☐
4. Has positive relationships with colleagues			
• Colleagues are satisfied with interactions.	☐	☐	☐
• Disagreements with colleagues are handled respectfully.	☐	☐	☐
• There are no ongoing conflicts with colleagues.	☐	☐	☐
5. Maintains good personal appearance			
• Dress, shoes, and nails are appropriate for the job of teaching young children (for example, sitting on floor and small chairs, lifting children, playing outside, messy activities, changing diapers).	☐	☐	☐
6. Maintains confidentiality			
• No gossip is generated about families and children.	☐	☐	☐
• No gossip is generated about colleagues.	☐	☐	☐
• Rules of confidentiality are used to stop others from gossiping.	☐	☐	☐
7. Has positive demeanor			
• Tone is positive.	☐	☐	☐
• Tone and language are respectful during disagreements (for example, no shouting, stomping, or threats).	☐	☐	☐

Family Survey

Dear family member,

As part of our teacher evaluation process, we ask parents for their feedback. All surveys are anonymous. We combine the results before we share them with teachers. Please put the completed survey in the envelope and put it in the Parent Survey box on the main desk. Thank you for your thoughts.

Name of teacher: _____ **Date:** _____

Center/school: _____

My child's teacher . . .	YES	SOMETIMES	NO	I DON'T KNOW
1. Has a clean and organized classroom.	☐	☐	☐	☐
2. Manages children's behavior well.	☐	☐	☐	☐
3. Has good rapport with my child.	☐	☐	☐	☐
4. Explains the curriculum to me.	☐	☐	☐	☐
5. Teaches my child social skills (sharing, politeness, caring, and so on).	☐	☐	☐	☐
6. Teaches my child academic skills (talking, reading, math, writing, and so on).	☐	☐	☐	☐
7. Provides fun and interesting activities to do and play.	☐	☐	☐	☐
8. Assesses my child's progress and tells me about it.	☐	☐	☐	☐
9. Communicates well with me.	☐	☐	☐	☐
10. Is friendly and helpful.	☐	☐	☐	☐
11. Is professional in dress and behavior.	☐	☐	☐	☐

I also want to say . . . (Please write any other comment you have below.)

From *Evaluating and Supporting Early Childhood Teachers* by Angèle Sancho Passe, © 2015. Published by Redleaf Press, www.redleafpress.org.
This page may be reproduced for classroom use only.

Coworker Survey

Dear staff member,

As part of our evaluation process we ask coworkers for their feedback. All surveys are anonymous. We combine the results before we share them with teachers. Thank you for your thoughts.

Name of teacher: _____ **Date:** _____

Center/school: _____

My coworker . . .	YES	SOMETIMES	NO	I DON'T KNOW
1. Has a clean and organized classroom.	☐	☐	☐	☐
2. Manages children's behavior well.	☐	☐	☐	☐
3. Has good rapport with children.	☐	☐	☐	☐
4. Explains the curriculum of our center/school.	☐	☐	☐	☐
5. Teaches children social skills (sharing, politeness, caring, and so on).	☐	☐	☐	☐
6. Teaches children academic skills (talking, reading, math, writing, and so on).	☐	☐	☐	☐
7. Provides developmentally appropriate activities.	☐	☐	☐	☐
8. Assesses children's progress and discusses data with coworkers.	☐	☐	☐	☐
9. Communicates well with me.	☐	☐	☐	☐
10. Is friendly and helpful.	☐	☐	☐	☐
11. Is professional in dress and behavior.	☐	☐	☐	☐

I also want to say . . . (Please write any other comment you have below.)

Performance Review Summary and Plan

Name: _____ **Date:** _____

We have reviewed three areas of performance: acts of teaching, results of teaching, and other professional behaviors.

Accomplishments (notes for each area of teaching, using the checklist):

Areas of growth (what the teacher needs to do to grow professionally):

Plan as the result of this meeting (SMART goals—may relate to one or more areas of performance):
1.
2.
3.

Teacher responsibility and timeline:

Supervisor responsibility and timeline:

Follow-up meeting on:

Post-Training Survey

Name: _____ **Date:** _____

Topic:

Two things (knowledge and skills) I learned that I want to use in my classroom:

    1.

    2.

Three things I need to make that happen:

    1.

    2.

    3.

Timeline. I would like to review these ideas and make a plan:

☐ NEXT WEEK   ☐ IN ONE MONTH   ☐ IN THREE MONTHS

Coaching Plan

Activity to be observed:

Tools used during the observation (such as children's data, videos, observation notes, and scores):

Last goal set:

Actual description of the observation and score, if appropriate:

Analysis of observation:

What happened? What does it mean for children's learning?

What needs to continue?

What needs to change?

New goal reflecting the analysis:

What is the desired result?

What will occur?

When will it occur?

Date for next observation:

Date for next post-observation meeting:

Mentoring Agreement

Mentor: **Date:**

Mentee:

Arrangements for meeting or contact

    When:

    Where:

    How:

Ground rules for working together

    1.

    2.

    3.

Main goals we are working on (no more than three)

    1.

    2.

Accomplishments

Initialed:

_____   _____

MENTOR   **MENTEE**

New Teacher Intake Form

Welcome to our center/school. We are very happy to have you on our staff. Please answer these few questions to help us get to know you better.

My strengths are:

I want to know more about:

I prefer communication by (check top two preferences):

☐ E-MAIL ☐ TEXTING ☐ WRITTEN NOTES ☐ BULLETIN BOARD ☐ IN PERSON

Two things very important to me in the workplace are:

When I am not at work, I enjoy:

Job Satisfaction Survey

Dear teachers,

I am checking in to see how our team is doing. From time to time it is important to slow down and reflect on our work together. Please respond to these ten statements by rating them with this scale. I will tabulate the answers and share the results at next week's meeting. Thank you for sharing your thoughts!

	ALWAYS	USUALLY	SOMETIMES	RARELY	NEVER
1. I am satisfied with my job.	☐	☐	☐	☐	☐
2. Staff meetings are useful.	☐	☐	☐	☐	☐
3. I feel respected.	☐	☐	☐	☐	☐
4. I am getting the help I need to do my job.	☐	☐	☐	☐	☐
5. My job is fun most days.	☐	☐	☐	☐	☐
6. I feel competent.	☐	☐	☐	☐	☐
7. We are a good team.	☐	☐	☐	☐	☐
8. I am clear on our goals for the children.	☐	☐	☐	☐	☐
9. Rumors and gossip are spread frequently.	☐	☐	☐	☐	☐
10. My daily work is manageable.	☐	☐	☐	☐	☐

I wish for more . . . (Please finish the sentence.)

I wish for less . . . (Please finish the sentence.)

References

Barnett, W. Steven. 2011. "Minimum Requirements for Preschool Teacher Educational Qualifications." In *The Pre-K Debates: Current Controversies and Issues*, edited by Edward Zigler, Walter S. Gilliam, and W. Steven Barnett, 48–53. Baltimore: Paul H. Brookes.

Bowman, B. T. 2011. "Bachelor's Degrees Are Necessary but Not Sufficient: Preparing Teachers to Teach Young Children." In *The Pre-K Debates: Current Controversies and Issues*, edited by Edward Zigler, Walter S. Gilliam, and W. Steven Barnett, 54–56. Baltimore: Paul H. Brookes.

Burchinal, Margaret, Marilou Hyson, and Martha Zaslow. 2011. "Competencies and Credentials for Early Childhood Educators: What Do We Know and What Do We Need to Know?" In *The Pre-K Debates: Current Controversies and Issues*, edited by Edward Zigler, Walter S. Gilliam, and W. Steven Barnett, 73–76. Baltimore: Paul H. Brookes.

Center for the Child Care Workforce. 2002. *Inside the Pre-K Classroom: A Study of Staffing and Stability in State-Funded Prekindergarten Programs*. Washington, DC: Center for the Child Care Workforce.

Child Care Aware of America. 2013. *Child Care Aware of America: 2013 State Fact Sheets*. Arlington, VA: Child Care Aware of America.

Copple, Carol, and Sue Bredekamp, eds. 2009. *Developmentally Appropriate Practice in Early Childhood Programs Serving Children from Birth through Age 8*. 3rd ed. Washington, DC: NAEYC.

Copple, Carol, Sue Bredekamp, and Janet Gonzalez-Mena. 2011. *Basics of Developmentally Appropriate Practice: An Introduction for Teachers of Infants and Toddlers*. Washington, DC: NAEYC.

Fives, Helenrose, and Michelle M. Buehl. 2010. "Motivation and Social Processes: Examining the Factor Structure of the Teachers' Sense of Efficacy Scale." *The Journal of Experimental Education* 78:118–34.

Fuller, Bruce. 2011. "College Credentials and Caring: How Teacher Training Could Lift Young Children." In *The Pre-K Debates: Current Controversies and Issues*, edited by Edward Zigler, Walter S. Gilliam, and W. Steven Barnett, 57–63. Baltimore: Paul H. Brookes.

Glickman, Carl D. 2002. *Leadership for Learning: How to Help Teachers Succeed*. Alexandria, VA: Association for Supervision and Curriculum Development.

Goffin, Stacie G. 2013. *Early Childhood Education for a New Era: Leading for Our Profession*. New York: Teachers College Press.

Harms, Thelma, Richard M. Clifford, and Debby Cryer. 2005. *Early Childhood Environment Rating Scale.* Rev. ed. New York: Teachers College Press.

Kagan, Sharon Lynn, and Rebecca E. Gomez. 2011. "B.A. Plus: Reconciling Reality and Reach." In *The Pre-K Debates: Current Controversies and Issues,* edited by Edward Zigler, Walter S. Gilliam, and W. Steven Barnett, 68–73. Baltimore: Paul H. Brookes.

Kauerz, Kristie. 2006. *Ladders of Learning: Fighting Fade-Out by Advancing PK–3 Alignment.* Issue Brief. Washington, DC: New America Foundation.

Kauerz, Kristie. 2010. *PreK–3rd: Putting Full-Day Kindergarten in the Middle.* Policy to Action Brief, No. 4. New York: Foundation for Child Development.

Korjenevitch, Maria, and Rachel Dunifon. 2010. *Child Care Center Quality and Child Development.* Cornell University Extension Project. Ithaca, NY: Cornell University.

Lutton, A., ed. 2012. *Advancing the Early Childhood Profession: NAEYC Standards and Guidelines for Professional Development.* Washington, DC: NAEYC.

McAfee, Oralie, Deborah J. Leong, and Elena Bodrova. 2004. *Basics of Assessment: Primer on Early Childhood Assessment.* Washington, DC: NAEYC.

MnAEYC (Minnesota Association for the Education of Young Children). 2004. *Minnesota Core Competencies for Early Childhood Education and Care Practitioners.* St. Paul, MN: MnAEYC.

Mooney, Carol Garhart. 2012. *Swinging Pendulums: Cautionary Tales for Early Childhood Education.* St. Paul, MN: Redleaf Press.

Morris, David. 2013. "Bill Gates Imposes Microsoft Model on School Reform: Only to Have the Company Junk It After It Failed." Accessed November 26, 2013 from www.alternet.org/education/billionaire-bill-gates-and-his-army -reformers-terrible-idea-bringing-ruthless-corporate.

NAESP (National Association of Elementary Principals). 2005. *Leading Early Childhood Learning Communities: What Principals Should Know and Be Able to Do.* Executive summary. Alexandria, VA: National Association of Elementary Principals.

NAEYC (National Association for the Education of Young Children). 2009. *Developmentally Appropriate Practice in Early Childhood Programs Serving Children from Birth to Age 8.* Position statement. Washington, DC: NAEYC.

NAEYC (National Association for the Education of Young Children). 2011a. *NAEYC Code of Ethical Conduct: Supplement for Early Childhood Program Administrators.* Washington, DC: NAEYC.

NAEYC (National Association for the Education of Young Children). 2011b. *NAEYC Code of Ethical Conduct and Statement of Commitment.* Washington, DC: NAEYC.

NBPTS (National Board for Professional Teaching Standards). 2012. *Early Childhood Generalists Standards*. 3rd ed. Arlington, VA: NBPTS.

Pianta, Robert C. 2011. "A Degree Is Not Enough: Teachers Need Stronger and More Individualized Professional Development Supports to Be Effective in the Classroom." In *The Pre-K Debates: Current Controversies and Issues*, edited by Edward Zigler, Walter S. Gilliam, and W. Steven Barnett, 64–68. Baltimore: Paul H. Brookes.

Porter, Andrew, Jennifer McMaken, Jun Hwang, and Rui Yang. 2011. "Common Core Standards: The New U.S. Intended Curriculum." *Educational Researcher* 40 (3): 103–16.

Protheroe, Nancy. 2008. "Teacher Efficacy: What Is It and Does It Matter?" *Principal*, May/June, 42–45.

Reagan, Timothy G., Charles W. Case, and John. W. Brubacher. 2000. *Becoming a Reflective Educator. How to Build a Culture of Inquiry in the Schools*. 2nd ed. Thousand Oaks, CA: Corwin Press.

Ritchie, Sharon, and Laura Gutmann, eds. 2014. *First School: Transforming Pre-K–3rd Grade for African American, Latino, and Low-Income Children*. New York: Teachers College Press.

Sabol, Terri J., S. L. Soliday Hong, R. C. Pianta, and M. R. Burchinal. 2013. "Can Rating Pre-K Programs Predict Children's Learning?" *Science* 341 (August): 845–6. www.sciencemag.org/content/341/6148/845.summary.

Sanders, William, and June C. Rivers. 1996. "Cumulative and Residual Effects of Teachers on Future Student Academic Success." University of Tennessee Value-Added Research and Assessment Center. Research Progress Report, November.

Schmoker, Mike. 2006. *Results Now: How We Can Achieve Unprecedented Improvements in Teaching and Learning*. Alexandria, VA: Association for Supervision and Curriculum Development.

Schweikert, Gigi. 2012. *Winning Ways for Early Childhood Professionals: Being a Professional*. St. Paul, MN: Redleaf Press.

Shareef, Intisar, and Janet Gonzalez-Mena. 2008. *Practice in Building Bridges. Companion Resource to Diversity in Early Care and Education*. 5th ed. Washington, DC: NAEYC.

Stronge, James H. 2007. *Qualities of Effective Teachers*. 2nd ed. Alexandria, VA: Association for Supervision and Curriculum Development.

Talan, Teri N., and Paula Jorde Bloom. 2004. *Program Administration Scale: Measuring Early Childhood Leadership and Management*. New York: Teachers College Press.

Tucker, Pamela D., and James H. Stronge. 2005. *Linking Teacher Evaluation and Student Learning*. Alexandria, VA: Association for Supervision and Curriculum Development.

US Bureau of Labor Statistics. 2014a. "Childcare Workers." *Occupational Outlook Handbook: 2014–15 Edition*. Washington, DC: US Department of Labor. www.bls.gov/ooh/personal-care-and-service/childcare-workers.htm.

US Bureau of Labor Statistics. 2014b. "Preschool Teachers." *Occupational Outlook Handbook: 2014–15 Edition*. Washington, DC: US Department of Labor. www.bls.gov/ooh/education-training-and-library/preschool -teachers.htm.

US Department of Education. 2009. *Race to the Top Program*. Executive summary. Washington, DC: US Department of Education.

Zaslow, Martha. 2011. "The Prekindergarten Debates: Contrasting Perspectives, Integrative Possibilities, and Potential for Deepening the Debates." In *The Pre-K Debates: Current Controversies and Issues*, edited by Edward Zigler, Walter S. Gilliam, and W. Steven Barnett, 73–76. Baltimore: Paul H. Brookes.

Zellman, G. L., Lynn A. Karoly. (2012) *Moving to Outcomes, Approaches to Incorporating Child Assessments into State Early Childhood Quality Rating and Improvement Systems*. RAND Corporation, Occasional Paper, retrieved September 1, 2014 from www.rand.org/content/dam/rand/pubs/occasional _papers/2012/RAND_OP364.sum.pdf

DATE DUE